Steven B. Wiley
with Jared Peatman, Ph.D.

To Mike,   8/21/2013

A Transformational Journey

Leadership Lessons from Gettysburg

May all your journey be bountiful

Published by:
Gettysburg Addresses, Inc.
8 Lincoln Square
Gettysburg, PA 17325

Kindest possible regards

Steve

To my late father, Richard, who told me I could do anything I wanted to do, and my late mother, Helen, who made darn sure I got it done!

To my wife Dr. Judy for having the capacity to balance me. Finally, to my three sons Benjamin, Nicholas, and Jeffrey, for bringing true joy into my life!

Contents

Introduction

Let him that would move the world, first move himself.
– Socrates

Everyone thinks of changing the world, but no one thinks of changing themselves.
– Leo Tolstoy

Over the last couple decades I've had the privilege of working with the majority of the Fortune 100 companies, scores of federal government agencies, and over 75 presidential appointees and their teams on leadership, followership, and organizational effectiveness. I can't begin to tell you how enlightening, enriching, and rewarding this has been. This book is about our experiences working with those professionals at The Lincoln Leadership Institute at Gettysburg, our human resource development company.

Before we begin I'd like to give you two minutes of my history, not to impress you, but to impress upon you that our approach is a little different. In the 1980s I started a company in my college town, Gettysburg, Pennsylvania, with $600 and a plan to restore the town's beautiful historic structures. There are a lot of historic buildings in Gettysburg and the business really took off. So we opened another office in Pittsburgh. That went well, so we opened another in Richmond. The next thing you know I owned the fastest growing franchise in North America, with 130 offices in three countries. I raised millions and millions of dollars in venture capital and was on the front covers of *Entrepreneur, Venture,* and *Inc. Magazine,* and on the front cover of *USA Today's* Money section. Life was good! That is, until 1989, when all of a sudden my little company lost $4.7 million. Think about that for a second. It wasn't my family's company, it wasn't the company I just happened to work for. It was the company I had started from scratch with $600. And in 1989 it lost $4.7 million.

In 1989, pretty much my full-time job was to lose money. Each morning I would say to my wife, "See you, sweetheart. I'm going to go lose some money. Be back about six, maybe seven." When you're losing $400,000 a month you can't pay your large bills. And when you can't pay your large bills the people to whom you owe several hundred thousand dollars don't go to collection agencies. They go see an attorney. So in 1989 I had 16 major litigations in 11 states and two countries with sixteen sets of my own attorneys, just to handle the correspondence in those respective states and countries!

And when you can't pay your big bills, obviously you can't pay your little bills either. In addition to the 16 litigations I had 387 accounts go to collection. Now, I don't know if you've ever had one bill go to collection because you couldn't pay it, didn't want to pay it, or refused to pay it, but collection agencies and lawyers make your life miserable. Multiply that misery by 16 litigations and 387 collection agencies.

To top that, on February 13, 1989, a day I won't soon forget, two IRS agents showed up and said, "We're from the Internal Revenue Service, and we're here to help." They started a TCA, a Total Company Audit, and they stayed for six and a half months. Ultimately the IRS demanded a quarter million dollars in additional taxes from the corporation, and $87 from me. What in the world was the United States Government going to do with my $87? It was during the peak activity for the space shuttle, so I used to envision a Cape Canaveral countdown going, "10-9-8-7. . . Wiley's check in yet? Hold off the launch! Hold it off!" Eighty-seven bucks, think of it. In 1989 I also had four root canals, my father died, my son went to neonatal intensive care, our cars were repossessed, and the bank started foreclosing on our house: it wasn't a particularly good year.

So I woke up one day and thought, if I'm going to survive I've got to become more effective at engaging and inspiring those around me to accomplish both my personal and our organization's goals. It was out of that experience, and the sudden, overnight really, realization of where I live and have lived since my freshman year in college, Gettysburg, Pennsylvania, that The Lincoln Leadership Institute was born. Gettysburg was the site of the largest land battle in North America. At the end of three days' fighting there were 51,000 casualties and perhaps 5,000 dead horses. There were six million pounds of flesh left on the fields when the armies marched away.[1] It was a scene of horror and desolation which humanity in all its centuries of existence had seldom seen. It was the occasion of the greatest amount of human suffering this country has ever witnessed.[2] I knew right then and there my situation was a cakewalk. Today's challenges are a cakewalk. 1863? Now that was a challenging time!

So for two decades I have been talking about leadership, followership, and organizational effectiveness in a **rapidly changing, stressful, frightening** environment, using the battle of Gettysburg as a metaphor.

Is it important that you are a good leader? Of course you know that I know that you know that it is! But sometimes I don't think we realize just **how** important it is. Let me cite two studies. Not surveys, but studies. There's a difference. Today anyone can run their own survey thanks to the Internet. A study is a little more scientific. Gallup asked 10,000 sophisticated decision makers, "What do you buy when you buy?" They responded, "We buy three things: the company or organization (Pfizer, Apple, Stanley Black & Decker), the product or service (a pharmaceutical, a computer, a power drill), and we buy the person we happen to be dealing with from that organization (a phone clerk, a salesperson, a CEO)." When asked which of those things was the most important, 86 percent of the respondents said… the person. Another study done by two of our clients, the White House and the Department of Labor, asked 6,000 decision makers, "Why do you stop buying? Why do you stop remaining loyal? Why do you decide not to get involved with an organization in the first place?" Two-thirds said it had nothing to do with money. Fees, rates, price, compensation, etc. And don't we love to use that as an excuse? "If only I could lower the price I would sell more product." "If only I could up the compensation I could get a more able person to assist me." Two-thirds said it was not because of quality. How can that be? I'll tell you how that can be: if you don't have good quality products and services you're not in business today, or at least you're not a threat to us. Two-thirds of the respondents said… it was due to a breakdown in the communication with the person with whom they were dealing.

---

[1] Drew Gilpin Faust, *This Republic Of Suffering: Death and the American Civil War* (New York: Alfred A. Knopf, 2008), 69.
[2] Gabor Boritt, *The Gettysburg Gospel* (New York: Simon & Schuster, 2006).

This gives me goose bumps. As we go through our lives and careers, 86 percent of the people who do what we need or want them to do will do so because of the relationship we bothered to cultivate with them. Two-thirds of the people who say "I'm just not going to do it," or "I'll be compliant, but I'm not committed," do so because we didn't bother to cultivate a relationship with them. We're in the people business. People buy from people, people follow people, people get ticked off at people, people fall in love with people.

Let me ask, how do you think we are doing at this thing called "leadership" in our country today? Are we very effective, moderately effective, not very effective? If you said "not very effective" or HORRIBLE, you're right. In 1992 Robert Kelley revealed that only one in seven employees think their boss is worth emulating, while J.C. Staehle found that the number one cause of employee dissatisfaction is a boss' failure to give credit. But bosses don't seem to get this! When an October 2011 Smartbrief poll asked, "How do you think your people would rate you as a leader?" over 74 percent of the respondents responded either "They think I'm the best leader they've ever had," or "They think I'm an above average leader." Less than five percent responded that they were below average!

Now why is that? Why is there so much room for improvement when it comes to leadership in our organizations?

In my experience there are three main reasons. First: who are we usually thinking about? Ourselves! Make no mistake about it, our ego is a huge drawback to establishing relationships with other people. Our mindset is "me me me me me me me!" It's all about what I want, what I got, and how I feel about it. It's "me me me me me me me" 24/7. Okay, enough about me, let's talk about you. How do you feel about me? So ego is a huge problem.

What other traits do we have that are not conducive to leading people? Are we very patient? Are we patient as a culture? No, we're impatient. When do we want results? Now! Instant gratification! Yesterday would be even better! Is that conducive to cultivating long-term relationships? Of course not.

Lastly, training and development budgets in North America are a major problem. Currently we spend over $100 billion on training and development annually. Of that money, 65 percent is spent teaching people the rules and regulations, policies and procedures, and if you have them, the features and benefits of your products or services. Are those things important? Of course! We have to know them. But aren't they the price of admission? Another 34 percent is spent teaching selling techniques. There's the hard close. The soft close. The repeat close. The repeat close. And my favorite, the surprise close: "Whoa! I wasn't going to buy any but that surprise close gets me every time, I'll take two dozen!" Where is the focus on leadership training?

Unfortunately you're not with us this week for a program, but this book will convey some of our messages and case studies. If you've already attended a program this will help you continue reflecting on the session; if you are thinking of attending, this book will give you an idea of the format we use and provide you with a few things to think about in the interim.

At the beginning of each case study we introduce a fundamental leadership concept. Not something overly complex, not with 15 different component parts, but a simple leadership concept. Then we follow the pedagogical steps of learning. I know what you're thinking: "Steve doesn't know the word 'pedagogical.'" It's a pretty big word, a five-syllable word. It's the second five-syllable word I learned – pedagogical and "your check's in the mail."

The first step is to introduce the concept. Then we illuminate the concept and bring it alive. When we're in Gettysburg we do this by going out to the battlefield and standing in the same places where human decision-makers changed the fate of their organizations and our nation. It's a powerful and moving experience for participants. Why this approach? We have it on good authority that adults don't want to be told how to think. Adults don't want to hear, "This is a great concept; go back and use it." Rather they say, "Show me. Let me think about it — let me understand if it's worthy of my time and let me decide if I can embrace it."

Fortunately, the process of standing on the battlefield almost always turns our participants into believers and immediately moves them to our third step: reflection. In today's world we rarely make time to proactively reflect on our lives. If all we do is go, go, go, do, do, do, act, act, act then we never allow ourselves the opportunity to reflect and improve. In fact, in a recent study 95-year-olds noted their second largest regret was not taking more time throughout their life to reflect. We need to make some time for this every day!

That leads us into the fourth and perhaps most rewarding step – application. Humbly this is why we've been so successful with our leadership program. Our leadership lessons and concepts are ones that you can apply immediately. So participants can ask, "What does it mean to me at Celgene, the Department of Homeland Security, New York Life, next week? What does it mean next Tuesday afternoon?" Social psychologists call that application process lateral or parallel thinking, and it is the key to everything we do.

So participants have a choice. They can say, "Hey, that's pretty interesting. I didn't know that Pickett's Charge was essentially the result of a mismanaged disagreement. When's lunch?" Or they can say, "That's interesting. What lessons from Gettysburg can help me improve my ability to make persuasive arguments at work, home, and in my community?"

The simple, strategic purpose for the time participants spend in Gettysburg is to encourage them, motivate them, stimulate them, provoke them — if necessary – to *think* – just to think. Think about your own leadership, your own followership, and the effectiveness of your organization. There is no better place in the world to do this than Gettysburg, for as Warren Bennis once said, "Like oarsmen, we generally move forward while looking backward."

A pharmaceutical sales team visited a few years ago and we discussed Abraham Lincoln's strategy for securing the 1860 Republican presidential nomination. Lincoln sent his committee to the convention in Chicago with instructions just to convince each state to have him as their second choice. Second! Not many sales forces today set a goal of being second best. But Lincoln knew that each state had their own favorite son whom they would not easily abandon. Rather than beat his head against the wall trying to be number one on every ballot, he essentially told his committee, "You go up there and try to get me to be everybody's number two, and then when their number one falters, I'll be in a position to move up." And that's exactly what happened.

Now, this pharmaceutical team could have moved on and gone home and told friends and family, "Hey, I learned how Abraham Lincoln got the nomination in 1860," and that would have been interesting cocktail party trivia. Instead, this team applied Lincoln's concept to develop a new sales strategy for their region. They looked at each other and said, "We've been making a mistake. We've been trying to sell our pharmaceuticals, our medical devices, our products to every doctor and hospital and clinic in our region to be number one on day one. We've got to learn from Lincoln.

"Some of our products are number one and we want to keep them there, just like Lincoln was the favorite son from Illinois. But for other products our clients prefer alternative companies. We have to change our strategy and aim for the number two spot for now, and then bide our time." And, by the way, even getting to be number two beats an awful lot of the competition. That's a terrific example of parallel and lateral thinking and how it can work for you. When this group left Gettysburg they were last in regional sales in North America. When they came back for our Level II program a year later, they were #1.

Now let me caution you: I have written this book as if I am speaking to you, so please forgive some of the informality, and the use of speaking rather than writing conventions. As you read it may help if you hear my voice in your head rather than see the words on the page. For those of you who have not met me, I promise I sound *just like* James Earl Jones. "Luke…"

For this book my friend and colleague Dr. Jared Peatman will provide some historical examples throughout to give you a sense of the way history enriches our understanding of leadership. Not only was Jared nominated by his district for history teacher of the year in Virginia in 2004, in 2009 he was named the most promising Lincoln scholar in the country. In 2012 Jared made good on that promise by winning the Hay-Nicolay Dissertation Award for the best work on Abraham Lincoln. Jared is a valuable member of The Lincoln Leadership Institute at Gettysburg faculty and has expanded our programs to the Alamo and Pearl Harbor.

With that we are off on our *Journey*! I hope you enjoy the book, and look forward to seeing you at one of our seminars sometime soon!

The most dangerous strategy is to jump a chasm in two leaps.
– Benjamin Disraeli

Chapter 1 — O Leader, Where Art Thou?

*Leadership is solving problems. The day soldiers stop bringing you
their problems is the day you have stopped leading them. They have
either lost confidence that you can help or concluded that you do not care.
Either case is a failure of leadership.*
– Colin Powell

*Treat a man as he is, and he will remain as he is; treat a man as he can
and should be, and he will become as he can and should be.*
– Goethe

At the beginning of our *Transformational Journey from Gettysburg* program
we ask participants to imagine they are in elementary school and the teacher
asks, "What is your definition of leadership?" What answer comes to mind?
"Leading other people?" But what would your best response be? Think of a very
simple definition. "Having the means to encourage people to follow you?" What
else? How about "getting people to let you in the front of the line?" Is that all it
is — getting people to accept your directions, no matter how valid? Think about
leaders of myth and history. The Pied Piper of Hamelin? He got people and rats
to follow him! Is that what you think of when you hear the word leadership?
Harry Truman once said that leadership "is the ability to get men to do what
they don't want to do, and like it." Does that one work better for you?

Confusing, isn't it? My favorite definition comes from Dudley Davis who
once said leadership is "the ability to create followship." Not fellowship,
followship. Every time I enter "followship" into my computer, the spell-checker
changes it to fellowship. Followship is the word I want. *Leadership is the ability
to create followship.* Wouldn't it be wonderful if the people around you, the
people you surround yourself with, followed you? Followed your advice, your

direction, your requests? And not just the people at work, but *everyone* around you? As Robert Kelley once said, "Without his armies, after all, Napoleon was just a man with grandiose ambitions."

We hope you will come away from this book with a few key ideas. Number one is to remember that leaders are not born, they're made. In fact they're self-made. I'll be talking about leadership training to a CEO of a company who earns a couple of million dollars a year and he'll say, "Steve, come on now, just between you and me, aren't people either born leaders or not?" I'll wonder how he made it to such a high compensation level, but then I'll remember the recent Gallup Poll that says 65 percent of the people who quit a job do so because of their direct manager. Leaders are not born, they are always self-made.

Let's look at this notion in more detail. How we are doing in America today when it comes to creating leaders? Are we good at it? Not so good? I'm afraid I've got bad news for you. We have tragically fewer leaders in America today than we did in the 1700s. When our founding fathers wrote the Declaration of Independence and Constitution we only had three million people living in America. And yet in Philadelphia, Pennsylvania, not too far from my home, six world-class leaders from different walks of life signed one or both of those documents. We had Washington, Jefferson, Franklin, Adams, Hamilton, and Madison. Over 235 years later we have 310 million people living in America and you can't name six world-class leaders. Who are you going to start with? I mean really, who are we going to name?

Now why is that? Perhaps partially because our generation has experienced more change than any other in history. Fifty years ago my grandfather taught me how to drive a car. When my youngest son was seven he taught me how to reprogram my VCR. That same year he asked, "Mommy, why is Daddy always bringing that briefcase home and going into that little room?" She explained very patiently, "Well, you know, Daddy doesn't have time to get all his work done during the day. So he has to put the remaining work in that briefcase and bring it home at night." And my son looked up and said, "Well, couldn't they just put him on a slower track?"

People living today have experienced more change than anyone else in history. The information revolution may very well be a development far more profound than either the advancement from hunter-gatherer to productive agriculture five hundred years ago or the movement from farms to cities in the Industrial Revolution. It seems impossible to gain perspective on the upheaval while in the middle of it, but we know something profound is going on. So what are we going to do about it? Accept that there can be no effective leadership method at this time? To use an academic word, "Baloney!"

Everyone reading this book has the potential to be a leader. Even an extraordinary leader. You don't have to be tall, you don't even have to be very smart. You can be whatever you are right now and be an incredibly effective leader. To illustrate good leadership vs. less effective leadership, let me tell you briefly about three American military commanders.

During the Vietnam conflict, in-country commanding General William Westmoreland received orders from Washington. His job was not to question them, just carry them out. His performance was evaluated on such things as body count. If you're old enough, you will remember seeing the daily body counts and kill ratios reported on the *Today* show. Vietnam was a troubling conflict: never before had America engaged in a war where killing alone seemed to be the end goal. The soldiers themselves were confused and bothered by the home-front opposition and General Westmoreland was being evaluated daily on such things as relative body count.

If the people in the headquarters tents couldn't question the mission, then the average foot soldier had no clue either. Imagine receiving your orders:

"Take that hill."

"Why?"

"I don't know."

"What happens if we do?"

"I don't know."

"What happens if we don't?"

"I don't know."

It was a war of missed missions, with a significant portion of the public unmercifully critical of the whole effort.

A young Norman Schwartzkopf served three tours in Vietnam between 1965 and 1970. Fate later placed him in charge of the coalition forces during Operation Desert Storm twenty years later. Now here is a difference worth noting: Schwartzkopf said, okay I'll command this effort, but I insist on being part of the strategy talks and in having all of my staff advisors with me in the room when the strategy is developed. Second, I want every single person who partakes in this conflict, from potato peelers on up, to know the plan and their part in it. Schwartzkopf understood that the days of a single vision dreamed up at the top and unflinchingly carried out are over, or as Warren Bennis asserts, "The Lone Ranger is dead!"

So we're talking about two very different scenarios, with two very different outcomes. Vietnam led to social tension, generational misunderstandings, and massive public distrust of the government that still has not completely gone away forty years later. The Gulf War ended swiftly in a resounding success in the terms of the military objectives that were sent forth. Afterward, soldiers returned home to parades and goodwill greetings.

Like Schwarzkopf, Colin Powell also served in both Vietnam and then oversaw Operation Desert Storm as the Chairman of the Joint Chiefs of Staff. Here is a man who has not only done it, but catalogued it in his book *My American Journey*, a smash bestseller that carries gems of wisdom on effective leadership. My favorites are:

- **You don't know what you can get away with until you try.** Good leaders don't wait for official blessings. They are not reckless, but they realize that if you ask enough people for permission, eventually someone will say, "No." So the moral is, don't ask permission when your gut says go ahead. I'm serious.
- **Organizational charts and fancy titles count for next to nothing.** The capacity to influence or inspire people is the real source of power, and it has little to do with placement on the organizational chart. People with drive, charisma, and concern for others will attract commitment regardless of their rank.
- **Great leaders are simplifiers who offer solutions everybody can**

understand. Effective leaders understand the KISS principle, or **K**eep **I**t **S**imple and **S**traightforward, to articulate vivid goals and values, and keep their visions lean and compelling. Their decisions are crisp and clear, not tentative and ambiguous. The result? Credibility and integrity for them, and the creation of followship.

· **Have fun – don't always run at a breakneck pace. Surround yourself with people who take their work seriously, who work hard, but also play hard.**

Seek to associate with people who have some balance in their lives, are enjoyable to spend time with, and have some non-job interests about which they are as passionate as their work. Avoid the grim workaholics.

The main lesson is that leaders must offer their followers a bill of rights. First, they have the right to be part of the strategy, to be involved in the strategy, to know what the heck the strategy is. They have the right to influence their own destiny. "What if we take the hill? What will happen?" They must know how taking that hill affects their own destiny. So explain the consequences if they do not follow your leadership.

A wonderful book called *Flight of the Buffalo* analyzes leadership among, you guessed it, buffalo. In a herd of buffalo, say two hundred head, how many of the animals know where they are going? One! If that lead buffalo takes a wrong turn and goes over a cliff, 199 other buffalo will hurtle over the cliff after him. You say, that's animals. But is it? In a flock of geese, how many geese know where they are going? All of them! They all know they're going to Ft. Lauderdale for the winter. When two or three break out of the pattern and die or disappear, the rest reconfigure and keep on going. Bringing this to the human world, a 1999 study found that in well-performing companies two-thirds of the employees understood the organization's mission and goals, while in underperforming companies only one-third did. I urge you to envision your followers as geese, not buffalo.

These procedures worked wonders with my three sons when they were growing up. By the time I came home Friday night after a week of travel my wife was ready for a break! One boy would want to play ball, another to visit the library, while the third would want to see a movie. So we would sit down on Saturday mornings and *together* come up with a strategy. And you wouldn't believe the balance of the weekend. They followed me around like little geese. First, we went to the movies. Then the library. Then to the ball game. They all cooperated because they were involved in developing the strategy. Odd as it sounds, involving people in the decision-making process ensures they are more likely to follow your leadership. Put differently, if you want people to buy in, you have to let them weigh in.

As the first step to involving everyone in the strategy decisions, a leader must define reality. When I sat down with my kids on Saturday morning, I let them know that traveling to Rome was not one of the options! Nothing is worse than unmet expectations: we can go to the library; we probably can't see the Vatican's archives this weekend.

At the end of all this planning what should we do? Say *thank you*. It's not difficult, you know. As Bennett Cerf once said, "A pat on the back, though only a few vertebrae removed from a kick in the pants, is miles ahead in results." This is not quantum physics, just basic common-sense human relations.

Do you know what the difference is between a manager and a leader? Managers do things right. Leaders do the right thing. So every once in a while pull yourself off whatever treadmill you are on and ask, "I know I'm doing things right, but am I doing the right things?" Only 27 percent of the companies in this country integrate their strategy and tactics. Which side of that equation do you fall on?

Was Lee Iacocca a good manager? He got fired, demoted, fired, demoted, voted out, and sued, so he wasn't necessarily a successful a manager. But he was one heck of a leader. When he presided over Chrysler the Big Three car manufacturers had been out of the convertible business for years because of safety issues. We just weren't making convertibles in the United States. Iacocca walked up to where a little hard-top car was coming off and made small talk with the engineer. The engineer gulped, my goodness, here is the big boss chit-chatting. Then Iacocca asked the $64,000 question: "How long would it take to make this model into a convertible?" The engineer thought for a moment and said, "Well, to do it right we'd have to send it over to Safety, then to Design, route it by Modeling, then schedule it for production. This could be a convertible probably in twelve to fourteen months." Lee said, "Well, I want to drive it home tonight as a convertible. I'll meet you here at five," and walked away. Just like that.

The engineer went to the bathroom, came back and hurriedly gathered a team of people with blow torches. They ripped the top off, covered the gash with masking tape and spray painted the chassis. Lee walked in at 5:05 p.m. and drove home in a convertible. On the ride, he wore glasses and a hat so no one knew who he was. But all he could hear and see were beeping horns and hands waving and thumbs-up signs. The next day Chrysler went into the convertible business. How did they do? Whoa! Massively well. Did any of the car makers follow them into the convertible business? Everyone did! The return to convertibles was a huge success!

In summary, leaders aren't born, they're made and almost always self-made. The first thing a leader has to do is define reality. You should surround yourself with people and allow them to be part of the strategy. You should allow the people around you to affect their own destiny. And at the end of the day, say thank you to anyone who has contributed to the success of your endeavors. That's pretty simple, and if you do it, you will create followship, from members of your family right through to your company and customers.

Creating Followers: Joshua Chamberlain and the 2nd Maine
by Jared Peatman

When I first started working with Steve I was thrilled to see he used Joshua Chamberlain as an example of an effective leader during the *Transformational Journey from Gettysburg* program. By way of introduction, Chamberlain was a mid-thirties professor at Bowdoin College in Maine when the Civil War broke out. [See image on page 51.] He joined the army in 1862, and a year later found himself commanding the 20th Maine Regiment at the Battle of Gettysburg. Chamberlain has gained almost cult hero status in the past twenty years due to his prominent place in Ken Burns' *Civil War* and the 1993 Ted Turner-funded movie *Gettysburg*.

Steve mentioned that leaders are not born, they are self-made. Chamberlain is certainly evidence of that sentiment. You may know that Chamberlain was a professor of rhetoric and modern languages at Bowdoin College when the war broke out. You probably don't know that this professor of, essentially, speaking, had to overcome a horrible stammer as a young man. So Chamberlain taught himself to speak in iambic pentameter, a rhythmic style that allowed him to work around his obstacle. Can you imagine how hard it would be to master speaking in iambic pentameter? After that, learning six new languages (including Swahili) was a cake walk.

When the Civil War broke out Chamberlain was pressured by both his family and Bowdoin to stay at home. By the summer of 1862, he could no longer resist the urge. He wrote the governor offering his services, but the state's Attorney General, Josiah Drummond, advised, "C. is nothing at all: that is the universal expression of those who knew him." Governor Washburn ignored this advice and offered Chamberlain the colonelcy of the 20th Maine. But knowing he needed more time before he would be competent to command the regiment, Chamberlain asked for and received the number two spot. How many people do you know would turn down a promotion because they perceived themselves not yet ready?

That turned out to be stroke of genius for all concerned. Adelbert Ames, a West

Point graduate and Medal of Honor awardee was put in charge of the regiment. For nearly a year Chamberlain learned military leadership both from Ames' example and all the books he could secure on the subject. When Ames was promoted to brigade commander in the spring of 1863, Chamberlain was ready to take over the regiment. While Ames had done a great job whipping the regiment into fighting shape, his transactional nature and reliance on positional authority to demand perfection from his men rather than inspire it in them had taken a toll.

From literally his first day in command it was clear that Chamberlain was different. On May 20, 1863, the day he was appointed colonel and took over the regiment, Chamberlain received word that as many as 180 mutineers from the 2nd Maine were to be assigned to his regiment. When these men enlisted they were told it was for two years, but the papers they signed said three years. Commanding General Joseph Hooker made the arbitrary decision that any man who had signed the three year papers by May 31, 1861, would only be held to two years' service, but anyone who signed them June 1 or later would have to stay for the extra year. [Aside: this was not effective leadership.]

Now this decision potentially had life or death consequences: 14 percent of the men in the 2nd Maine had died during the first two years of the war, and of the 100 men who were ultimately transferred to the 20th (we'll get to that in a minute) 41 had already been shot!

Not surprisingly, the men mutinied and refused to do duty. They were arrested, placed under guard, and denied food. These were big, strong woodsmen, mariners, and miners, and after three days they showed no signs of breaking. It was then that corps commander George Meade sent the entire group to the 20th Maine and told Joshua Chamberlain he could deal with them in any way he saw fit, up to and including executing the whole lot!

In addition to the large group of men who were transferred en masse (as depicted in the Ted Turner production *Gettysburg*), other small groups of men also trickled in throughout May and June. Chamberlain met with each group as they arrived, listened to their problems, and tried to win over their hearts. The letter Chamberlain wrote to Governor Abner Coburn on May 25, 1863, gives us great insight into his leadership:

The transfer of the "three years men" of the 2ⁿᵈ Maine has been so clumsily done, that the men were allowed to grow quite mutinous – left uncared for in their old camp after the 2ⁿᵈ had gone for several days, & having time and provocation to work themselves up to such a pitch of mutiny that Gen Barnes had to send them to me as prisoners, liable to serve penalties for disobedience of his orders. You are aware, Governor, that promises were made to induce these men to enlist, which are not now kept, & and I must say that I sympathize with them in their view of the case. . . . They need to be managed with great care & skill; but I fear that some of them will get into trouble for disobedience of orders or mutiny. My orders are to take them & put them on duty – which they have already refused to Gen. Barnes & others. I shall carry out my orders whatever may be the consequence; but I sincerely wish these men were fairly dealt with by those who made them their promises.

Two days later Chamberlain wrote the governor again, noting, "I have taken a liberal course with them, because they are nearly all good & true men, but I shall be obliged to carry a firm hand. They are now ordered on duty, & their orders must be carried out. They are expecting to hear from you, in reply to a communication of theirs & their expectation of this keeps them in an undecided state of mind as to doing duty."

In his handling of the 2ⁿᵈ Maine men, Joshua Chamberlain illustrates perfectly Steve's steps to creating followership. First, he defined reality: he could not allow the men to go home, they simply had to serve that extra year. But it is quite clear from the letters that he took their pulse, heard their concerns, even passed one of their letters along to the Governor, and thus involved them in the discussions and decisions about their future. His comment that they were "good & true men" echoes an earlier letter in which he asserted that the addition of the 2ⁿᵈ Maine veterans would make the 20ᵗʰ the best regiment from the state. Perhaps most importantly, throughout this process we see a Chamberlain who did the right things for the right reasons. He did not buy the "ends justify the means" mindset that his higher ups and predecessor all-too-frequently employed, but instead followed his personal values.

So what was the result? Transferee John O'Connell later wrote, "We got around all right owing to the Disposition of Col Chamberlain and the officers of the Regt to treat us well." In a July 20 letter Chamberlain revealed that all but six of the mutineers had agreed to do duty before Gettysburg, while three picked up rifles and rejoined the ranks during that battle. Ultimately two more would do the same, leaving only Henry Moore as the outlier Chamberlain sent to prison. To my everlasting shame, Moore is from my hometown. A 99 percent success rate is pretty impressive.

When the 20th Maine arrived at Little Round Top on July 2, 1863, 100 of their 500 men were from the old 2nd Maine, and they made the difference that day. The 20th was ordered not to give up their ground, but their line swayed and nearly broke a half dozen times before Chamberlain, out of ammunition, ordered his men to make a bayonet charge that finally repulsed the Confederates and secured the position. Without those 100 extra men it seems unlikely Chamberlain could have persevered. For his, "Daring heroism and great tenacity in holding his position on the Little Round Top against repeated assaults, and carrying the advance position on the Great Round Top," Chamberlain was awarded the Medal of Honor.

But the story doesn't stop there. Chamberlain knew he wasn't the only one who deserved to be recognized for gallantry on Little Round Top. One of those mutineers-turned-comrades was a man named Andrew Tozier. As a teenager Tozier ran away from home and took to the sea, remaining there until enlisting in the army. He was wounded twice before Gettysburg, and had twice been in Confederate prisons. Showing his faith in the new men, Chamberlain asked Tozier to be the regimental color bearer just a few days before the battle, and the veteran accepted the post despite the personal danger it entailed. (Several units at Gettysburg lost up to ten color bearers over the course of the three days.) In recommending Tozier for the Medal of Honor, Chamberlain wrote, "At the crisis of the engagement this soldier, a color bearer, stood alone in an advanced position, the regiment having been borne back, and defended his colors with musket and ammunition picked up at his feet." When the final charge came, Tozier was at the fore.

But the war was hard on Andrew Tozier. Between a head wound, several missing fingers, and a disabled shoulder, this former laborer could not find work. Desperate, he joined a cousin in a plot to rob a bank. Caught and charged with armed robbery, Tozier was looking at a life in prison until the governor gave him a full pardon, brought him home and tutored the veteran in reading and writing as a step toward gainful employment. When none was forthcoming the governor hired Tozier to work for him. That governor? Joshua Lawrence Chamberlain. From a runaway to a mutineer to a bank robber, the only times in his life when Tozier held it together was when he was around Joshua Chamberlain. And for his part Chamberlain never forgot that without Tozier and his comrades the 20th Maine would have either been annihilated or disgraced on Little Round Top. Ten years later he had the opportunity to say thank you in a most profound way.

As a leader, our number one goal is to create followship. Our first step, as Steve is fond of saying, is remembering it's not about us, it's all about the mutineers. Few Civil War leaders were better at creating followship, even out of mutineers, than Joshua Lawrence Chamberlain.[1]

---

[1] Thomas Desjardin, *Stand Firm Ye Boys From Maine: The 20th Maine and the Gettysburg Campaign* (New York: Oxford University Press, 2009).

Reflection — O Leader, Where Art Thou?

Our strategic purpose here is not to preach at you, but just to encourage you to think and reflect about your own leadership. Toward that end, the following questions might be useful.

Reflect…

- Do I rely too much on my positional authority to get things done?

- Do I effectively involve the people around me in the decision making process?

- Do I properly set the stage by defining the reality for those around me?

- Do I, as Dale Carnegie suggested, give sincere appreciation to those around me?

… and Apply

- What can I do this week to increase the willingness of people to follow me?

- What is one existing issue that I can jointly work through with those around me?

- In what area do I need to proactively define the reality for my followers?

- Who are three people to whom I can offer sincere and specific praise for things they have done in the past week?

- Do I have mutineers in whom I need to find value?

Chapter 2 — Mindsets as Assets

Success is not the result of spontaneous combustion. You must set yourself on fire.
– Reggie Leach

In addition to the *Journeys* program we host in Gettysburg, I've had the privilege of speaking on "The Human Side of High Performance" to most of the Fortune 100 companies. I call it the "Human Side" because despite all the technical skills we might have, all the advances in technology over the last few decades, and the incredible number of techniques we have for doing our job, in the end it all comes down to mindset and how we approach the people we interact with, be they clients, colleagues, bosses, subordinates, or family members.

There is a lot of weight on our shoulders as representatives of our companies. So let's talk about increasing our own productivity — the results we get. Take the pressure off yourself as an individual for a moment and let me ask you — how are we as a nation doing at influencing others? Are Americans pretty effective influencers? My friend, we as Americans are probably the least effective influencers on the planet. How can that be?

The main answer seems to come out of the post-World War II era when we were the only industrial country left standing intact. Think about it, an American company came up with a great product, spent enough money on advertising, and *boom*, you had a successful car, *boom*, you had a successful pill. Whatever the product, it was a success. If it was dog food, there was always a dog out there to buy it. In that environment, Americans could afford the luxury of being order takers. Just be at the right place at the right time and make your quota.

This is no longer the case. Now we have competition, serious competition, throughout the globe. Purchasing agents have fiscal responsibility. Customers want to hear from your CFO what your internal costs are. We no longer can afford the luxury of just being order takers.

What happens to companies that get complacent? They cease to exist. Of the companies on the original Forbes 100 list in 1917 only 40 were still in existence by 1987, and only 18 were still in the top 100. As of today just one, General Electric, has outperformed the stock market, the average, over that time. We must adapt or die.

Why are we such poor influencers? Partially because of the hectic pace of modern life, or the sheer variety of options available at any one time, we have become incredibly impatient. When you make a comparison with other world cultures, we in America probably have the least patience on the planet. Patience isn't even regarded as a virtue in this country, although it is highly respected in places like Asia and the Middle East. Then you go to one more level: the difference between men and women.

If you're a man in America today you are the most impatient creature on God's earth. And if you don't believe that and you are a guy, think about the last time you rode in an automobile as a passenger when a woman was driving. I can hear you now. "Run the light, run the light, run the light, ahhh, you could've made it! Ahh, that truck wasn't that big. Now we have to sit here for a whole minute! Damn! If only I hadn't lost my license."

We are categorically impatient. When we want to conclude a deal as quickly as possible, that's not conducive to a sale. If all we want is to get in, score, and get out, we're not going to build any sort of relationship with the client. Patience is the forgotten virtue in America. It goes hand in glove with another undervalued character builder beginning with the letter p – persistence. All other things being equal, the patient, persistent individual will succeed over the jackrabbit, competitive, hardball player virtually every time. Let's just say that persistence can't be fully realized without patience.

Learn the art of patience. Apply discipline to your thoughts when they become anxious over the outcome of a goal. Impatience breeds anxiety, fear, discouragement, and failure. Patience creates confidence, decisiveness, and a rational outlook, which eventually leads to success.
– Brian Adams

A few years back *USA Today* published the results of a poll in which a thousand random people were asked to name their favorite movie actor. Perhaps it was the phrasing of the question, but no female actors landed in the top ten. Most of the names in the top ten were predictable enough — DeNiro, Nicholson, Newman, Ford, and so on, but guess who was number one? And not by a little — but by a very wide margin? John Wayne! Imagine, John Wayne, who passed away in the 1970s and hasn't made a movie in a generation, was number one by a landslide. Even today John Wayne still holds the third spot! That speaks volumes about our culture.

Take, for example the busy professional, imbued with the American cultural influence, including a heavy dose of John Wayne movies. Maybe he's feeling a little insecure one day because his company is behind schedule. It's fight or flight. The person he's negotiating with has actually become an enemy in terms of psychological transference. So he plays hardball and metaphorically beats the other guy to a pulp, landing a lopsided agreement that will look great back at the office.

But wait — if I just beat you to a pulp today, what's going to happen tomorrow? Either you will refuse to see me or you'll spend the rest of your life trying to get back at me. Negotiating by engaging in battle — aggravated by impatience and the ego-fueled competitive instinct — fails miserably. Patience is a virtue. It always has been, and always will be. Competitiveness may be fine on a football field, but when it translates to a zero-sum "if you win therefore I lose" mentality, it will sabotage results.

It is quite possible, and always desirable, for both parties in a transaction — or any other human interaction — to come away winners. When one party comes away feeling beaten and suckered, how will that contribute to the renewal of a positive business relationship over the long term? Obviously it won't — if anything it will start a cycle of injury, revenge, retaliation and ultimately the loss of an opportunity to do more business. Checking your ego at the customer's door and leaving the win-lose mentality behind allows you to pay more attention to what your customer needs and wants, with much better results. Later in the book, we will give you a technique for doing this called "Listen Until It Hurts."

So, here we are, culturally impatient and prone to behave on the ego plane, the dimension where one must win and one must lose, the zero sum arena. We have no choice but to pay attention to the consequences of these actions and to change these traits at the level where they do the most damage: within our own heads.

Oftentimes the only difference between screaming success and mediocrity is just an additional five minutes of perseverance.

The competitive nature of our companies' business has changed and will continue to change in the next millennium. The bad news is that we're not really effective leaders and influencers given our cultural and psychological baggage and the fact that corporate training and development in America concentrates on the wrong thing. The good news is that we can change it. We said earlier that two-thirds of the people who stop doing business with your company do so because of a breakdown in communication. Now here are the never-refuted results of a 1971 study by Albert Mehrabian:

- Only 7 percent of communications is *what* you say: features and benefits, reasons to buy, any other technical information about the company.
- 38 percent of communication is *how* you say it: the tone of your voice.
- 55 percent of communication is *physiology*: your posture, your facial expression, your body language.

Wow! Ninety-three percent of communication has nothing to do with features and benefits. Not sure you buy it? Years ago a group of Syracuse psychologists analyzed news coverage of the 1984 presidential election and made a startling discovery. Without knowing their part in the experiment, viewers noted that while Dan Rather and Tom Brokaw wore "happy" expressions the same amount of time when talking about either candidate, Peter Jennings appeared happy a third more often when speaking of Reagan than Mondale. A subsequent survey found that those who primarily watched ABC, Jennings's station, were approximately 19 percent more likely to vote for Reagan than viewers of either CBS or NBC! Wow! Physiology matters, ladies and gentlemen.

If you concentrate on that 93 percent it will profoundly affect your ability to get your way — possibly for the first time. That doesn't mean you should ignore the 7 percent, the features and benefits part of communication. But knowing those is the price of admission. You don't need us to help you understand how your own business products work. But maybe we can help you with the other 93 percent of communication, which is by far the most important.

What you are speaks so loudly I cannot hear what you say.
– Ralph Waldo Emerson

Profound Silence: The USS Arizona Memorial
by Jared Peatman

To summarize Steve's main point, American leaders could be more effective if they paid greater attention to the role of both interpersonal relations and non-verbal communications in leading. A picture truly does paint a thousand words, so let's think for a minute about the power of non-verbal communications as shown through the monuments we erect to the past.

As a nation, we have spent a great amount of effort commemorating and memorializing the past. Over time the shape and style of our national monuments have changed: the obelisks favored in the nineteenth century gave way to the enclosed domes of the early twentieth while today's architects are fond of incorporating water. Like Albert Mehrabian, however, designers in all periods have understood that the verbal messages they can convey on these monuments are dwarfed by the non-verbal cues visitors internalize. Few sites better exemplify this dynamic than Pearl Harbor, Hawaii.

While there are many excellent sites in Honolulu that deal with the attack on December 7, 1941, when most say the "Pearl Harbor Monument" they refer to the *USS Arizona*, the famed battleship that was bombed and sunk by the Japanese. Of the 1,400 crewmen, 1,177 were killed that day, and over 1,102 remain entombed in the ship.

While a million people a year visit Pearl Harbor, and 4,500 tickets are given out every day for the *Arizona* monument, but only 200 people are allowed on the memorial at a time. After touring the visitor center, travelers to the memorial today must take one of the navy shuttles from the main part of the island out to the site adjacent to Ford Island, a short but significant ride of a few hundred yards. This ride across the harbor mentally prepares visitors for what they are about to experience, so by the time they arrive at the memorial there is a calm and quiet about the group that stands in contrast to the energetic masses that swarm the visitor center. [See images on page 52.]

The designer of the memorial noted that the peak at one end of the memorial indicates American pride and confidence before the attack, the low point in the middle shows the national depression as a result of the attack, and the peak on the opposite end represents a revitalized and victorious America in 1945. That the entire memorial is white reminds visitors that this is now a peaceful site, in great contrast to the confusion and suffering that pervaded in 1941.

As visitors stare down at the wreckage of the *Arizona*, oil seeps up to remind us that this event is not so very far in the past. Perhaps we remember the old saying, "The price of peace is eternal vigilance." Looking past those oil streaks to the decks of the ship below, one cannot help but think of the 1,100 men entombed just a few feet away. Perhaps because the deceased sailors are unseen their presence seems magnified. Many visitors arrive expecting to see a battleship; all come away realizing they have just seen a national cemetery.

When visitors look up from the water to take in their surroundings they first encounter large cement structures noting where the other ships were moored that fateful day. With a sense of the *Arizona* story, visitors are shocked by the realization that the terror on that ship was not in isolation, but part of a larger whole. Those with an active imagination can see the Japanese bombers coming over the mountain rim to the west like a dark cloud, streaking toward Pearl Harbor, looking for their pre-determined targets, and dropping bomb after bomb before breaking off the attack and returning to their carriers.

However, Peal Harbor is not about defeat, but rather victory. Since 1999 the *USS Missouri* has been docked within sight of the *Arizona*. A massive ship, it was on the decks of the *Missouri* that the Japanese formally surrendered on September 2, 1945. Thus, within sight of one another are the places where, for America, World War II both began and ended. The *Missouri*, half again the size and speed of the *Arizona*, represents not only American victory over the Japanese, but American progress as well during those four years.

The most amazing part about the *USS Arizona* memorial is that this entire message is presented non-verbally. Sure, there are words on the memorial, from a listing of the names of the men on board the ship to the markers of the other ships along "Battleship Row," but these words are not what draw the emotion and craft the story told at the *USS Arizona* memorial, rather it is the non-verbal cues that have transformed some rusted out metal into one of the most sacred spots in America today.

Malcolm Gladwell revealed that most people make up their minds about someone within two seconds. TWO SECONDS! A typical person can speak only seven or eight words in that amount of time, so clearly our evaluation is not based on what they said but rather their non-verbal communication. When you enter someone's space, what non-verbal symbols do you look for? Perhaps more importantly, when someone enters your space, what non-verbal signals are you sending them? We've probably done some intentional things like putting up pictures of family, our degrees, maybe some awards. But what about the unintentional messages we are sending? What is the totality of our message? And most importantly, is that really the message we want to send? Gladwell went on to note that 80 percent of the time the impression students form of their teacher within the first two seconds of class remains unchanged at the end of the semester. You really do only have one chance at a first impression, and that chance is clearly a non-verbal opportunity. Let's make the most out of it.

Reflection — Mindsets as Assets

Our strategic purpose here is not to preach at you, but just to encourage you to think and reflect about your own leadership. Toward that end, the following questions might be useful.

Reflect...

- What type of relationships do I have with my clients and colleagues?

- How patient am I in dealing with those around me?

- How often does my ego get in the way of my relationships?

- What is my main strength in the area of non-verbal communications?

... and Apply

- What can I do this week to improve my relationships with my clients and colleagues?

- Which of my clients or colleagues seem to be drifting away from me? What can I do to reestablish that personal relationship?

- What is one thing I can do to improve the effectiveness of my non-verbal communications?

Chapter 3 — Mission: Success

You are not here merely to make a living. You are here to enable the world to live more amply, with greater vision, and with finer spirit of hope and achievement. You are here to enrich the world. You impoverish yourself if you forget this errand.
– Woodrow Wilson

The inscription on the Temple at Delphi admonished visitors to "Know Thyself." The master psychologist Carl Jung observed that to "know ourselves" may be the ultimate purpose of life. Before serving as a resource to other people, there is an exercise you can work on whose payoff is incredibly valuable. I'm talking about designing your very own mission statement.

When I ask audiences, "How many of you have a mission statement?" often not one hand goes up. These aren't small rooms, either. The organizations, whether Apple, L'Oreal, or FedEx, all have incredible mission statements. But the employees don't have personal mission statements. That's the problem. So if you don't have one, you are not alone. (Once someone raised his hand and said that his personal mission statement was, "To make more money." This is not what I mean.)

Personally, I had to grow up a lot before developing a worthy mission statement. My mission statement is to provide the most powerful leadership training in the world, and to do so in an entertaining way. I want to have a profound impact on each and every individual in each and every audience — to make heroes of people who have me speak to their companies or join us in Gettysburg, and world-class resource people of the audience. That's my mission statement. It may sound grandiose, but instead of your mission statement being "to make a hundred calls today," or "to make more money this month than last," why don't you try a mission statement that says, "I'm going to solve my client's problem. I'm going to make my client a hero at his or her organization today." That's a mission that will help inspire you each and every day.

Let's consider an alternative to calling yourself a "leader." Let's broaden our self-definition and think of ourselves instead as "Consultative Resource Professionals." If you had business cards that said "Consultative Resource Professional" do you think more clients would call you? Do you think more of your subordinates would feel comfortable coming to you when they need guidance? I suspect they would.

When you stretch yourself a bit and think of your mission statement as more global, as encompassing other people, it works wonders. It may sound corny, but as soon as my focus became profoundly impacting an audience and making heroes out of the people who brought me into their organizations, things began to click for me. You need to focus on how your work can benefit other people, not simply your own bottom line. If you do that, you're going to make friends with the people you deal with and enter beneficial and lasting partnerships with them. That's the pinnacle of empowerment.

Stephen Covey's ground-breaking book, *First Things First*, uses the adjective "empowering" to describe a proper, personal mission statement. He says an empowering mission statement represents the deepest and best that is within you. If there is anything worth pondering, reviewing, memorizing, and writing into your heart and mind it will be your mission statement. I hope if you do not yet have one, you will begin to work on one while reading this chapter.

Covey grabs attention by asking readers to envision their 80th birthday. Try to imagine a wonderful celebration where relatives, friends and people from all walks of life come to honor you. Yes, honor you. The point of the exercise is to visualize what each of these people would say about you, one by one: the qualities of character they would remember, outstanding contributions they might mention. What difference would you have made in their lives? This exercise can give you tremendous insight into the potential power and passion of your life's vision. Visualize your eightieth birthday celebration. What an idea!

Covey contends we all lead three lives. We have our public life at work or social or community events. We have our private life with our friends and family. And then we have our deep, inner life. This deep inner life is largely hidden, even from ourselves if we let it stay so. But it is in this deep inner life, this secret life, where we detect our life's mission. We don't invent a mission for ourselves so much as discern what it is from among our unique combinations of talents and preferences and within the specific opportunities we have in life.

Before going further, we need to discard two false assumptions that many people hold. The first is, "my job is my mission." Your work may *express* your mission, but your mission is always larger than your job, because it reflects ultimately who you are as a person. Second, "I'm not important enough to have a mission." This is nonsense. Everyone has an impact on the universe. If you don't believe that, go watch *It's A Wonderful Life.*

A powerful mission statement taps directly into the fire within you. It gives you the courage and confidence to break from the norm and exert your independent willpower toward a noble end. Rather than react to a trend or behaving instinctively, a powerful personal mission statement encourages you to exercise free will, depart from the herd, and become both more self-reliant and disciplined. It is in the exercise of our free will that we become truly human. I can hear you say, "Big deal, humans can develop the will to do anything." But without the passion of vision, discipline is merely regimentation, isn't it? Isn't it a drudgery? A whitenuckled, grit-your-teeth approach to life? Who wants that?

In *Good to Great* Jim Collins notes that great companies ask three questions when establishing their "Hedgehog Concept," which has a lot of similarities to the mission statement for an individual. Those three questions are: 1) at what can I be the best in the world?; 2) what drives my economic engine?; and 3) about what am I deeply passionate? An empowering mission statement, like a great company's Hedgehog Concept, describes your personal gifts and expresses your unique capacity to contribute to the greater good. It's comprehensive and based on principles. It addresses the physical, social, mental, and spiritual dimensions of life. It deals with all the significant roles in your life because what you're looking for is *balance* in personal, family, professional, and community roles. Does this sound like a tall order?

Oh, and one more thing: it is written to inspire *you*, not to impress anyone else. Your mission statement should fit your own consciousness of yourself. Not my view of you, not your mother's view of you, not your boss' view, not the view of your parole officer, if you have one. Nor does it have to fit the things and events from your past. It should be oriented by the present and point to the future. The past is gone. In fact, if the past has brought problems that may be good news. It is a powerful moment indeed when you realize you are unhappy or frustrated with a life situation and vow to change, develop energy, and improve the situation.

The other key elements of a mission statement are pretty straightforward. It has to be written down, and in the present tense. I *am* a resource professional, not I'd *like* to be a resource professional. The statement should include vivid descriptions covering a variety of activities. It should be inspiring, exciting, clear, engaging, and it should be specific to you. You have enthusiasm, gifts and unique talents, so it should showcase these. It should cover both your work and your personal life. Get the impression this will take a certain amount of work? Remember the words of Socrates: "The unexamined life is not worth living."

Once you have put the required effort into formulating your mission statement, reading them is like standing on sacred ground. The statement reveals your important inner priorities. And the payoff is immediate, because truly meaningful mission statements create energy and commitment. Energy is the source of motivation. Energy is empowering.

Having a mission statement makes personal time management far easier, too. No longer is it necessary to compile longer and longer daily to-do lists. Unless the task fits your mission, it probably shouldn't get that much priority. It's that simple. Jim Collins, who we introduced a minute ago, notes that great companies (and individuals) are highly *un*diverse in their activities; rather they focus on the few things they can do at a truly exceptional level.

In *The Path*, Lori Beth Jones says a good mission statement needs only three elements. It should be no more than a single sentence long. It should be readily understood by a twelve-year-old, and you ought to be able to recite it at gunpoint! So, keep it short, keep it simple, and keep it memorable. The only unsuccessful mission statements are low-energy – the ones that do not inspire us because they are bland — or those that are unintelligible to a twelve-year-old. If you use the outline below, you should be able to arrive at a meaningful, vibrant statement for your mission.

Now let's look at goal setting as a separate activity. Once we have a mission statement we need to construct goals so we have a road map to success. The old saying "if we fail to plan, then we plan to fail" may be cliché, but it's also true. The purpose of goals is to provide a mental target to hit.

Some goals require that we gain some skill instruction, that we have someone teach us how to do certain things. I once took a course in auto mechanics, figuring it would be fun to learn how to fix up my '66 Mustang. Eighty percent of the class dropped out after two lectures because the course required math homework. Their motivation wasn't strong enough to carry them through the hurdle. They wanted to tinker with an engine block, but not for any real purpose. Now, suppose there was a young student in the classroom with a mission statement to become a certified auto mechanic. Do you think a little arithmetic homework would stop that person? Of course not. The passion and commitment of the mission statement help keep us motivated despite the obstacles we may find. Personal excellence and progress toward challenging goals are not easy to attain. But after developing a mission statement, each of us can embark on the journey — and enjoy the learning, the plateaus, and the ride along the way.

Nothing can take the place of determination in goal setting or in life. We need to have a mission statement that will to boost our persistence to go on no matter how crushed, defeated, or demoralized we may become. If we keep putting one foot in front of the next in service of a worthy mission, then perseverance and the law of averages will see to it that we succeed with time. Persistence and the power of will are the essential factors in translating goals into reality, the indomitable traits. Persistence, strength of will, and a passionate mission: what an unstoppable combination!

Setting goals requires an action plan. Once you develop the habit of writing and rewriting your goals, you can update and improve them as you go along. The more time you spend on this, the better and more believable the goals become. It's as if the repetition burns them into your subconscious and makes you chase after them relentlessly, even while you sleep. In fact, reading over your goals just before bedtime activates your subconscious and puts it to work for you overnight. Often ideas will present themselves the next day, as if by coincidence. Setting goals yields a very high return on the time we invest — perhaps higher than any other activity.

Taking action without planning is a source of most of life's problems because we then do things without considering the long-term consequences. The converse is also true: the most successful accomplishments are preceded by a well-designed plan. The more complete and aligned the plan, the more likelihood for success. The more completely you imagine and visualize the outcome, the greater the chance it will be fulfilled in your life. Don't be afraid of daydreams. Embrace them and put them to work for you.

Once we have a mission and a plan, perseverance is the only thing standing between us and success. I took my son to a Baltimore Orioles game a few summers ago. While he was eating a hot dog, I read the program and realized something about the difference between a journeyman and an All Star player. A batter who gets five hits every twenty at bat has a .250 average and makes $500,000 per year. Another player who gets six hits every twenty at bat has a .300 average and makes *$4 million* a year. It may not seem like a lot of difference in performance: one hit in every twenty at bats, but it results in massively different compensation.

Genius is an infinite capacity for taking life by the scruff of the neck.
– Katharine Hepburn

Small differences in results also create dramatic differentials. Most of these differences are due to perseverance. The famous 80/20 rule or Pareto Principle says that 20 percent of your activity accounts for 80 percent of your accomplishments. In his classic best seller *Think and Grow Rich* Napoleon Hill startled readers with his discovery that we become what we think about most of the time. Successful people do not dwell on mistakes or failure. They don't worry uselessly about the past. They focus on their aspirations, their dreams, their objectives, and their goals. If you think more often about your own mission, your dreams, your goals — and less about what you don't have — watch what happens.

More recently Gallup research into strengths-based leadership has confirmed and extended Hill's research, showing that employees who use their top five strengths on a daily basis are six times more likely to be engaged at work than those who do not.[1] The Gallup folks suggest that trying to improve our weaknesses rather than leveraging our strengths is taking the path of *most* resistance. But this is not a new revelation: over two hundred years ago Benjamin Franklin said unused talents were as useful as sundials in the shade!

When you develop goals, especially written goals, you begin to lead a purposeful life. Your energy focuses like a laser beam. You overcome obstacles. You are harder to distract. Defense Department studies of prisoners of war indicate that those with no defined missions or goals were the most susceptible to brainwashing. Prisoners with centering influences, on the other hand, were stubborn resisters. They understood the long-range consequences of giving in, and thus they did not crack. They may have been physically injured from torture and abuse, but their will was indomitable.

I hope you won't ever undergo torture. But with goals and a mission statement, you will be unlikely to founder on the rocks of some work competition — or the jealously of a professional rival. Roy Disney had it right when he said it was easier to do the right thing when you know ahead of time what you stand for. Keep your goals and purpose front and center and watch your progress soar. Of course your goals should have benefits that extend beyond just yourself. Unless your activity is somehow a benefit to others, it is not likely to succeed. Personal happiness can never be a goal because happiness is the logical outcome or byproduct of striving for a purposeful goal. I'm fond of the notion that the road to heaven *is heaven*, or alternatively, "It's not the pursuit of happiness, but the happiness of pursuit."

Now let's see where we are in this. I mentioned that your goal should benefit not only you but others. What do others want? They want security, comfort,

---

[1] Tom Rath, *Strengths Finder 2.0* (New York: Gallup Press, 2007), iii.

love and respect. Well, my goodness, let's give it to them. And you can achieve great success in the process. Here are my rules for success as envisioned in your mission statement and goals.

- **I: Dream big!** Set high, challenging goals for your work and personal life. Big dreams give you the energy to take big action. Imagine you could increase your team's productivity ten times. If you keep repeating the new amount to yourself over and over, it sounds more real. Repeat it until it becomes your reality.
- **II: Do not dwell on failure, that will only paralyze you to inaction.** The average self-made millionaire has been broke two or three times, including me!
- **III: Persist until you achieve.** Your ability to persevere will become the single greatest index of your self-esteem. Sometimes the only difference between mediocrity and screaming success is an additional five minutes of perseverance.
- **IV: Do what you love to do.** If you won $5 million tax-free tomorrow, what sort of work would you choose to do for the future? Your answer speaks volumes about your personal area of excellence. Until you work in this area of personal excellence you cannot throw yourself into what you do with enough passion to increase your earnings ten times.
- **V: Resolve to learn from your mistakes.** Extract every possible lesson from each experience and strengthen yourself.
- **VI: Ask others for help; don't go it alone.** Develop and nurture a support network.

Setting goals and having a mission leads to success. Successful people go beyond the point where the average person would stop, and they are willing to do what most will not do. Writing out your mission statement will activate forces that will draw success to yourself.

If you want to be truly successful invest in yourself to get the knowledge you need to find your unique factor. When you find it and focus on it and persevere your success will blossom.

Missions: A Path to Success or Failure
by Jared Peatman

– Sidney Madwed

Every time I heard Steve speak about the tremendous importance of mission statements my thoughts turn to the historic sites we use for our programs and the extent to which strong or weak mission statements and goals affected the outcomes at those places. Let's look briefly at the Alamo, Pearl Harbor, Normandy, and Gettysburg to see the effect of mission statements and aligned goals on real historic endeavors.

The massacre at the Alamo offers one of history's clearest examples of the perils of not developing a clear, motivating mission statement. For years Mexico encouraged American settlement on the Texas frontier as a way of populating the region, but by 1830 it was apparent that the Americans were clearly oriented toward Washington, D.C. instead of Mexico City. As a result Mexico banned further immigration from the United States, announced it would no longer turn a blind eye to the importation of slaves, and made clear the intention to begin enforcing the collection of customs. The revocation of all land grants in 1835, at the same time customs officials were seizing merchandise, set the state ablaze. On October 2, 1835, men under William Barrett Travis attacked the Mexican garrison at Gonzales and the revolution began.

Three months later the Mexican garrison at Bejar, or San Antonio, fell to the Texians. Now the Texians encountered real problems. Fighting not for independence but for a return to the policies of the 1820s, the Texians had adopted a mission that was reactive rather than proactive. By not declaring independence as their mission, which was clearly the path most ultimately wanted, the Texians handicapped the goals they could set and actions they could undertake to bring about that end. After defeating and pushing back the two main Mexican garrisons, the various volunteer commands literally did not know what to do. In early January commanding General Sam Houston ordered San Antonio abandoned and the Alamo blown up, but resident Jim Bowie thought it important to hold the city, and led the volunteers he commanded into the old mission-turned-outpost. The rest, as they say, is history.

Legend has it that the men at the Alamo nobly scarified themselves to buy time for Houston to assemble and train the rest of the volunteers. Unfortunately, that is simply not true. Houston was negotiating with the Cherokees for the first five days of the siege, and did not issue an order for the volunteers to concentrate until March 9, three days after the Alamo fell. The defenders of the Alamo were sacrificed not in pursuit of a worthy mission, but rather due to the inaction the *lack* of a clear mission brings to all in its path.

How might things have been different had the leaders of the Texas Revolution established a clear mission of independence in October 1835 and then set goals to achieve that mission? If they rigorously asked whether every action advanced the mission, would they have allowed 200 men, including three of their best leaders and most of their cannon, to face off against an assault force of nearly 2,000 men? Likely not.

In contrast to the Texas Revolution, the planners of the D-Day invasion in Normandy had a clear mission and made sure every action advanced that mission. Dwight Eisenhower best expressed that mission in his note to the Allied Soldiers on June 6, 1944: "You will bring about the destruction of the German war machine, the elimination of Nazi tyranny over the oppressed peoples of Europe, and security for ourselves in a free world." Talk about an inspiring mission! It also meets Steve's criteria: it focuses on the contributions the team members will make to the larger world, it is empowering, it is inspiring, it is in the future tense, and it is simple. [See image on page 53.]

For two years Eisenhower worked toward that vision of a world freed of Nazi tyranny and oppression, and it was anything but easy. British Prime Minister Winston Churchill wanted to launch a series of smaller invasions to harass German forces and allies throughout the world, but Eisenhower resisted. He knew that you couldn't destroy Germany by fighting in far flung locales. He agreed to Operation Torch in North Africa in order to hold together the alliance and also to train and test his men, but he never lost focus of the larger mission. From North Africa the Allies jumped to Italy, but Ike insisted that no materials needed for Normandy be diverted to

Italy, and left partway through the Italian campaign to begin organizing the invasion of France. He faced continued pressure to divert his attack plans; Winston Churchill favored a move into southern France, not northern, while Joseph Stalin wanted more direct help for his beleaguered soldiers in the east. Eisenhower once referred to all the dickering as "the transatlantic essay contest," but he knew an invasion of Normandy was the single task most likely to advance his mission, so he persisted despite the obstacles. Along the way Eisenhower created an innovative organization that literally invented new technology to better carry out the mission, including new types of landing craft and artificial harbors.

On June 6, 1944, the months of planning came to fruition as 156,000 soldiers, 5,000 ships, and 11,000 planes attacked Normandy and established a position from which the Allies would march to victory in less than a year. By keeping everyone's eyes on a clear, impassioned vision and ensuring that all goals and tasks advanced that mission, Eisenhower led the Allies to ultimate triumph.[2]

If you find yourself in an organization that either does not have a clear mission or is struggling to align their goals to advance a mission, the Union war effort and leadership of Abraham Lincoln in 1863 offers hope! Throughout the first two years of the war the North sputtered along, ostensibly fighting for union but knowing that a victory which brought a simple return to the pre-war status would be nothing more than an armistice. Historians continue to debate whether the Emancipation Proclamation in 1863 was the first step in announcing a new mission — the *creation* of a better union, one without slavery — or simply the addition of a powerful goal/task under the existing mission of *restoration* of the preexisting union. From a leadership perspective the difference does not matter: by *either* announcing a new, powerful mission, *or* by establishing a powerful goal that would ultimately advance his existing mission, Lincoln showed us that we can make a mid-course adjustment to improve our mission and the alignment of our goals with that mission. At Gettysburg, in November 1863, Lincoln even more powerfully stated the mission, and in so doing put the nation on a moral high ground that paid

[1] Geoff Loftus, *Lead Like Ike: Ten Business Strategies Form the CEO of D-Day* (Nashville: Thomas Nelson, 2010).

political and diplomatic dividends.

The lesson, in the end, is to *Remember the Alamo!* But remember that the organizers there failed largely because they had no compelling mission statement that drove their actions. Alternatively, on D-Day, Dwight Eisenhower's leadership ensured that the 156,000 men involved in the Normandy invasion achieved meaningful goals that advanced a larger mission that they all knew and believed in. Lastly, Abraham Lincoln's redefinition of the mission in 1863 gave the Union armies the strength and will to see the war through another two years of fighting and persevere to ultimate triumph, giving us all hope that we, too, can right the ship.

Reflection — Mission: Success
Mission Statement Worksheet

The implications of having a mission statement can be rather daunting. You may have to acquire new skills. Some people may even need to relocate, because our geographic surroundings must be naturally and positively aligned with our desired achievements. (You can't be a Wisconsin trail guide in Gettysburg, Pennsylvania). But the penalty for not making a mission statement is even more scary, because not to have one leads to confusion and lagging self-esteem. Either you are living out your own mission or you are living someone else's. It's your choice.

The Mission Statement
What Is It, Anyway?

A written-down reason for being.
– Steven Covey

So simple a twelve-year-old should understand it.
– Laurie Beth Jones

Though you must work toward self-knowledge before discerning your mission statement, you will find it is amazingly simple to write it down once you get started. It only takes some people a few hours. When you have a mission, it may broaden over time. That's perfectly okay. The immediate payoff is that you achieve *clarity* — *clarity* of the type that makes everything easier; from goal setting to time management.

Passion and excitement are the keys. Here's the best way to begin: Think about what most excites you or makes you enthusiastic. Ask yourself what sorts of things do you dwell upon most of the time in these areas: Family ... Work ... Health ... Relationships. List them on a sheet of paper.

Next, *think of three action words* that really hit your hot button ... words like "teach," "motivate" "solve," or "generate." Think of your own action words and write them down. Then, *think about what principle or activity you would be willing to devote your life to.* For some, this brings to mind a key phrase or value like "joy" or "service" or "family" or "creativity" or "excellence" or "computers." Write down a word or phrase for yourself.

The last piece of this puzzle will be *to think of the group, entity or cause you most would like to help in a positive way.* "Labor relations," "women's issues," "the environment," "fashion," "biotech," "public safety," "health care," "business clients," "the news," or whatever you want to write down.

Once you get this done, go back to your action words (three verbs), add your core values, and for whom it is intended and . . . *Voila!* You will have the basics for your mission statement.

Using the pieces of information you brought to light by performing the exercise on the prior page, write your personal mission statement in the space below.

Write it in the present tense, describing the kind of life that you want to lead based on the positive qualities and values you have identified. Ready?

My Mission is to _____, _____, *and* _____
(your three verbs) _____ *(your core value or values) to, for, or with*
_____ *(the group or cause which most excites you).*

Does the statement you wrote surprise you? Does it fit you? How do you feel when you say it out loud? A good mission statement will be exciting, inspiring, clear, and engaging. It will be specific to you and to your enthusiasms, gifts, and talents. If this isn't the case with your statement, then re-work it until it meets the criteria. Get a thesaurus and find better words. Make it resonate. Keep at this until you can explain the sentence to a twelve-year-old and say it in your sleep.

BONUS
The "WOW" Questions

Here are some provocative questions to help you ponder what it means to become your own person, to discern your true inner nature, and to develop the will to act on your knowledge of self:

1. Where am I now in my life?

2. What meaning does this exercise have in the context of my life as a whole?

3. What is trying to emerge within me at this time? What potential is trying to unfold?

4. Which self images and beliefs of the past must I relinquish to support whatever it is that is emerging from within me?

Reflection — Mission: Success
Goal Setting Worksheet

When properly used this worksheet will give you information that can enable you to overcome any obstacle toward achieving your goals. A good way to perform the entire exercise is with pen and paper. A better way is to find some privacy and allow yourself at least two hours. The best way is to treat yourself to a day of solitude to think and reflect — quietly and calmly — about your answers to these questions. Do this exercise with candor and diligence; it may very well change your life. This is personally sacred material. Treat it as such and receive boundless rewards from completing the exercise. Ready?

Warm Up
Get a Glimpse of Your Potential

1. If you could eavesdrop on people talking about you, what would you hope to hear?

2. What does your answer to the previous question prompt you to change about yourself?

3. What are your major excuses for not making this change before now?

4. What are remaining situations in which you blame others for your own lack of success?

Now You're Baking
Rise to the Challenge

1. If you had no fear of failure, what would you make a point of doing?

2. If the opinions or approval of others didn't matter, what would you do differently?

3. What are your own positive qualities?

4. What negative qualities would you rather not have?

Situations Must Not Rule You
Taking Responsibility

Whatever the mind can conceive and believe, it can achieve.
– Brian Tracy

You feel positive about yourself to the degree you feel you are in command of your own life. *What parts of your life do you feel are most and least under control?*

You can trace every condition in your life back to a specific cause. *How has cause-and-effect worked in your family, career, health or financial situation?*

Whatever you believe with intense feeling or deep set emotion becomes your own reality. Thus, what you expect can become a self-fulfilling prophesy. *Is what you strongly believe in helping you or hurting you?*

You must inevitably attract into your life people and situations that are in harmony with your dominant thoughts. Your outer world is a mirror image of your inner world. *Everything that is in your life today you have attracted to yourself. Are you satisfied with your circumstances and the people around you, or should you make some changes? If so, should you change the people and circumstances, or should you go to work on changing yourself? How?*

Your Subconscious Mind
A Gold Vein Ready to Be Tapped

Compile a "dream list" of things you would want to see in your life, if only you could believe they were possible to achieve. Please remember that there are no limits to the list. This list is only for you, and no one else, to see.

Modeling
A Skill to Move You Rapidly Toward Goals

1. What three people – living or dead – do you most admire? *Why?*

2. List the qualities of character you admire in others and would like to possess yourself.

3. Rank those qualities you admire in the order of your personal priority.

4. What would you do differently as a result of this information?

Success
Goal Setting Accelerates It

1. Setting goals has already brought you success to a moderate degree. To demonstrate this, list three goals, large or small, that you have set for yourself and achieved thus far in your life.

2. Now, write your answer to this next question *in no more than one minute:* Currently, what are your three most important goals in life?

3. What would you do, where would you go, and how would you spend your time if you learned today that you have six months to live?

4. What would you do and how would you change your life if you won $5 million in tax-free cash tomorrow?

5. What one great thing would you dare to dream *if you knew you could not fail?*

6. In what areas do you currently have the greatest intensity of purpose?

7. What beliefs are most important to you? Why?

8. What is your individual area of excellence?

9. What will you do differently because of your answers to these questions?

Achieving Clear Goals

1. What is one major, definite goal in your life at the present time?

2. Write down this goal using SMART criteria (Specific, Measureable, Attainable, Realistic, Timely).

3. Now write down a detailed plan for achieving your goal.

4. What are the possible obstacles standing between you and your goal?

5. Choose one obstacle and describe, step by step, what you can do to overcome it.

6. List possible sources of help and support.

Chapter 4 – Stretch Your Style!

We don't see things as they are, we see things as we are.
– Anais Nin

Once you have a mission statement, developing an understanding of personality styles — your own and your customer's — is a core competency of great value. Earlier we established that knowing the "features and benefits" of your organization is the price of admission. Now let us concentrate on your own personal features and benefits. Let's tally the distinctive assets we have as individuals and think of these as the features and benefits of our own personality.

You've likely heard of the Myers-Briggs Type Indicator, a psychological profile that places you in one of sixteen groups based on the personality you exhibit. You learn to estimate where other people fit within the profile and how you can best communicate with them. The problem is that I have all these features and benefits of my products and services to remember, *then* I have my 16 possible personalities, *then* the 16 possible personalities those I interact with could have. That adds up to 256 combinations! Talk about sensory overload!

All too often people take the Myers-Briggs test and conclude they have the fundamentally wrong personality for the position they hold, or aspire to hold. This is nonsense. Whatever your personality type, you can become a world-class leader. Whether you are reserved or outgoing, it doesn't matter. Embrace your fundamental personality; just know that there are different types out there, and resolve to try to relate to them.

Our personality, the way we chose to reveal ourselves to the external world, is a product of parental expectations, rules, socioeconomic status, and lots of other diverse influences. Strike up a conversation with a fellow passenger on a plane or a train, and pay attention to how that person describes himself or herself. People usually define themselves in terms of roles. "I am the HR specialist for the Pentagon," or "I am an HR specialist temporarily working for the Pentagon while preparing for something better to come along." Or "I'm a young mother juggling the demands of career, home and children." Or they say, "I'm a real friendly, outgoing type." Or "I'm kind of reserved and very thoughtful." All of these are descriptions drawn with references to externalities.

Personality type is pretty much a given, but you can modify your personality style. What if I asked you to make ten new friends today? How would you go about it? What if you had a goal to enter into five new partnerships this week? The Insight Inventory is a useful tool that analyzes four areas of your personality that I think matter when it comes to effectively communicating with people.

- The first is how you get your way — directly, indirectly, or somewhere in between. It doesn't matter if you're direct or indirect, but it's important to know which you are.
- Secondly, you're either outgoing, reserved, or in between.
- The third area is how you pace activity. You either have a sense of urgency — got to get it done yesterday — or you're steady — you ponder, compare, and contrast. Either way is perfectly acceptable. It is just important to know which style you lean toward.
- Finally, how do you manage details? Are you precise? You've got to computerize, categorize, and alphabetize. Or are you unstructured? Where's my hat? Has anyone seen my keys? Whether precise or loosey-goosey, the only thing that matters is that you know what tendency you have.

How do you get your way? How do you respond to people? How do you pace activity? How do you handle details? Instead of fretting over sixteen personality types, now you only need to consider these four areas. You need to know these things before you get up in the morning, because if you're calling someone who is unstructured and you are highly structured, or you wish to visit someone who is reserved and you're outgoing, or you go to a meeting with someone who wanted everything done yesterday, and you want to compare and contrast for five minutes, it will be like speaking two different languages.

Remember, you are in charge of communication. Since 93 percent of communication has nothing to do with features and benefits, it's vital to find out how your style will match or conflict with that of the person you are dealing with. It's professional suicide if you don't know personal styles.

Let me give you an example of the benefits of understanding style and personal communication preferences. My wife, Dr. Judy Wiley, has a Ph.D. in psychology, and has been analyzing me ever since we got married. I'm pretty sure her initial interest in me was as a test subject. But I digress. A few years ago, at her suggestion, we both took the Insight Inventory test and compared our results. It only took us seven minutes to take the test and seven minutes to correct it, but it served as the best marriage counseling we've ever had. I'm talking about maybe two years of counseling in fourteen minutes. We found out we're on opposite ends of the chart in every one of these categories.

I'm very direct; she's indirect. I'll be watching television, and she'll come down and say, "Steve, we're out of toilet paper." Five minutes goes by and she'll say, "Steve, did you hear me? We're out of toilet paper." Now does she mean we're out of toilet paper? No, she means go get some toilet paper. Now I'm a little more direct. When I say, "We're out of toilet paper," I mean we're out of toilet paper! You're on your way to the bathroom? You better grab a newspaper because we're out of toilet paper.

When it comes to pacing, I'm a wreck, I've got to get it done yesterday. I have this constant sense of urgency. Not her. It took me 15 years of marriage to realize that when my wife says, "Let's go look for a couch this weekend," we might not find a couch. When I go looking for a couch, I'm going to buy it, bag it, and drag it back. So although we're on opposite ends of the chart, by learning to stretch our styles, life has improved!

Every person you encounter is a unique combination of these four traits. And yet our tendency is to conduct ourselves in the same manner all day long. Of course you're going to want to know the style of those around you. Sometimes I'm asked, "How do I know what their style is? I took the test, they didn't!" I say shame on you if you don't take the time to get to know the people around you to find out whether they're more outgoing than reserved; more precise or unstructured. We're not talking about selling vacuum cleaners door-to-door. We're talking about cultivating relationships. Some people want to shortcut the system and know which of each type is more common, but nationally the numbers break down pretty evenly. We might have to stretch our style four, five, six or ten times a day. And yet we tend to go through our day making the same style of presentation.

My favorite example is of an urgent type dealing with a steady type. Slow decision-making drives the urgent type up a wall, while pressure to hurry a decision causes the steady person to balk. It's a classic, almost comical situation, if it were not so true to life.

We often conduct ourselves differently at home than we do at work, which is further evidence that we can adapt our style. You may want to conduct yourself differently on the second call than you did on the first call. The third call you may want to stretch your style again based on your better understanding of the other person's makeup. Embrace your personality, don't try to change it — just stretch your style.

If you are an indirect person, and you wish to better communicate with a direct individual, try being a little more assertive. Appearing unsure, hesitant, or tentative will lead Directs to think you don't have the knowledge you should. If you are a Direct dealing with an Indirect, be aware that your self-assurance and strong convictions may appear arrogant to them.

If you're outgoing, be sensitive to the reserved person's need for quiet time. If you're a Reserved dealing with an Outgoing, think about being a little more enthusiastic or animated in talking than you would prefer. Otherwise they may misinterpret your reserve as a lack of interest.

There are different things you can do to stretch your style. My wife and I are a perfect example of how you can improve communication. For an Urgent to better communicate with a Steady, you need to be more patient. Don't push. Give advance notice. If you're a Steady dealing with an Urgent, present your ideas quickly and succinctly and be ready to take action. If you can't make a quick decision, at least let them know you are thinking about the issue.

If you're an Unstructured and you want to better communicate with a Precise, you should get your facts and details together before trying to persuade a Precise. And if you have set up a meeting, ensure that you are on time. If you're a Precise and you're dealing with an Unstructured, don't bring up too many details. Don't try to enforce too many rules too quickly, and avoid excessive perfectionism.

Please use these tips as a resource to measure your style and connect with someone at the level of their style. It's all part of waking up in the morning to the understanding that we should be resource people, not leaders and salespeople. We need to have our own personal mission statement. We know the kind of assets we have. We know how to adapt our style so that it synergizes with the people around us.

"It's not what you look at
that matters,

it's what you see."

— Henry David Thoreau

Joshua Lawrence Chamberlain
Commander of the 20th Maine at Gettysburg

USS Arizona
December 7, 1941

USS Arizona Memorial
Present Day

SUPREME HEADQUARTERS
ALLIED EXPEDITIONARY FORCE

Soldiers, Sailors and Airmen of the Allied Expeditionary Force!

You are about to embark upon the Great Crusade, toward which we have striven these many months. The eyes of the world are upon you. The hopes and prayers of liberty-loving people everywhere march with you. In company with our brave Allies and brothers-in-arms on other Fronts, you will bring about the destruction of the German war machine, the elimination of Nazi tyranny over the oppressed peoples of Europe, and security for ourselves in a free world.

Your task will not be an easy one. Your enemy is well trained, well equipped and battle-hardened. He will fight savagely.

But this is the year 1944! Much has happened since the Nazi triumphs of 1940-41. The United Nations have inflicted upon the Germans great defeats, in open battle, man-to-man. Our air offensive has seriously reduced their strength in the air and their capacity to wage war on the ground. Our Home Fronts have given us an overwhelming superiority in weapons and munitions of war, and placed at our disposal great reserves of trained fighting men. The tide has turned! The free men of the world are marching together to Victory!

I have full confidence in your courage, devotion to duty and skill in battle. We will accept nothing less than full Victory!

Good Luck! And let us all beseech the blessing of Almighty God upon this great and noble undertaking.

Dwight D. Eisenhower

General Dwight Eisenhower's D-Day Message

The David Wills House in Gettysburg
The location where Abraham Lincoln finished the Gettysburg Address
and home to Steven B. Wiley's Lincoln Leadership Institute

Tomorrow We Must Attack
Dale Gallon

"The ultimate measure of a man is not where he stands in moments of *comfort and convenience,* but where he stands at times of *challenge and controversy.*"

— Martin Luther King, Jr.

Why Do We Remember "Four score and seven..."?
by Jared Peatman

Earlier Steve mentioned Colin Powell's comment that great leaders are simplifiers, and that is certainly true. Also true is that great leaders are great communicators. The number one key in effective communication is realizing, as Steve and Joshua Chamberlain have taught us, it is not about us, it is all about the mutineers.

We call Ronald Reagan "the Great Communicator," and he well deserves that reputation. But few presidents have been better able to reach a diverse number of communication styles, both in different settings and even within a single speech, than Abraham Lincoln. Have you ever asked yourself why it is that the Gettysburg Address is the most famous and most memorized speech in the world? Did you know that two foreign nations, China (now Taiwan) and France, both literally based their governments on Lincoln's famous speech? In 1963 Secretary of State Dean Rusk noted that the "central commitments of the American experiment are probably known to more people in other lands through the words of the Gettysburg Address than those of the Declaration of Independence." How is it that *that* speech, not any one of a number of other contenders, has so resonated with people around the world?

The answer, quite simply, is that Lincoln intuitively understood that you have to be aware of people's personal communication preferences *if* you want to actually communicate with them rather than simply make words in their general direction. Some people want you to be brief and cut to the chase, others want you to provide the rationale behind your decisions and thought processes. Some people simply want to know what decision you have come to, others want to also know all the alternatives you discarded along the way.

Are you one of those people who wants to cut to the chase and make a decision quickly, the type of person who reads the first line in an email and then stops if you think you have the gist of what is to come? If so, you probably appreciate the Gettysburg Address, for you can get away with simply reading that first line: "Four score and seven years ago our fathers brought forth on this continent, a new nation, conceived in liberty and dedicated to the proposition that all men are created equal." On the other hand, if you are someone who wants more detailed information, the type of person who actually reads your company's strategic plan, then you too likely admire the Gettysburg Address for Lincoln explains the past ("the brave men, living and dead, who struggled here"), the present ("we have come to dedicate a portion of that field"), and the future ("we here highly resolve that these dead shall not have died in vain").

If you want to simply know the way forward, Lincoln provides that, "We take increased devotion to that cause for which they gave the last full measure of devotion." Some are happy knowing simply where you plan to drive the bus, others want to check every footnote to make sure your plan is based on verifiable information and that they agree with that route and destination. Lincoln provides that too, both in his citation of the Declaration of Independence and in his assertion that "government of the people, by the people, for the people, shall not perish from the earth."

Whether he knew it or not, at Gettysburg Lincoln ensured the continued popularity of the Gettysburg Address by appealing to all communication types. Is there a way you can follow Lincoln's model to increase the number of styles you reach in your daily communications?

Reflection – Stretch Your Style!

Reflect...

- Am I direct or indirect? Reserved or outgoing? Urgent or steady? Precise or unstructured?

- Have I, in the last week, unrealistically expected someone to conform to my style?

- Have I, in the last week, consciously adapted to someone else's style?

... and Apply

Think about someone who you will interact with this week during an important meeting.

- Do you think they are direct, or indirect? How should you moderate your style to accommodate them?

- Are they reserved or outgoing? How should you moderate your style to accommodate them?

- Are they urgent or steady? How should you moderate your style to accommodate them?

- Are they precise or unstructured? How should you moderate your style to accommodate them?

Chapter 5 — Listen Until It Hurts

Listening, not imitation, may be the sincerest form of flattery.
– Dr. Joyce Brothers

When you are trying to develop a relationship, asking the right questions is a far more valuable technique than explaining features and benefits of your products, yourself, or your organization.

There are books on start selling, stop selling, and every other kind of selling the authors can define. Most of them are based on writings from the 1920s. We're facing millennial challenges with procedures developed nearly a century ago. Great. The only thing that they seem to agree on is that the sales process consists of four categories: the preliminaries, the probing question/explanation of features and benefits, problem solving/solutions, and yeah, you guessed it, the close.

Ten thousand sales professionals were asked which of those four categories is the most important. Do you want to guess what they said? The close. And that's right if you're selling vacuum cleaners door to-door. But not when you're trying to cultivate relationships.

So their second guess was … *ta-da* … features and benefits, features and benefits; if it's not the close it must be features and benefits. But focusing on features and benefits leads us into a trap. The client says, "I'd like a blue one."

We say, "We've got a red one and a green one."

"That's great. I'd like a blue one."

"We've got an orange and purple one."

"But I'd like a blue one."

"We've got a round one and a square one."

So it must be the preliminaries, right? After all, you don't get a second chance to make a first impression. Yes, if you're just selling door-to-door you don't. But if you're cultivating a relationship, the duration of your sales cycle might be a week, a month or years.

It doesn't take a brain surgeon to figure out the most important category: the probing questions you ask. Last year corporate America spent $1 billion — that's a thousand million dollars — teaching sales professionals in North America the difference between a close-ended and an open-ended question. And you know what? It doesn't make any difference.

There is, however, a style of questioning that will profoundly affect your ability to sell. Before we start talking about the most important component of selling, the inquiry, we have to make sure that when you ask questions, you listen to the answers. Most of us think we're good listeners. In my case, I thought that was one of the few things I did well until one rainy day when my wife said, "Steve, you're not a very good listener."

I said, "Judy, I have a lot of flaws, most of which you've already pointed out to me, but the fact is, I'm a pretty good listener."

She said, "No, you're not."

I said, "Yes, I am."

She said, "Well then, listen to this." And she read me following paragraph.

A business person had just turned out the lights in the shop, when a man appeared and demanded money. The owner opened the cash register. The contents of the cash register were scooped up and the man sped away. A member of the police force was promptly notified.

So I said, "Okay, what's your point?" She said, "You didn't hear me." I said, "I heard you." She said, "But you didn't listen well." I said, "I heard every word you said." She said, "Just in case, I'm going to read it to you again." So I'm going to ask you to read it again, too.

A business person had just turned out the lights in the shop, when a man appeared and demanded money. The owner opened the cash register. The contents of the cash register were scooped up and the man sped away. A member of the police force was promptly notified.

Okay? Don't look back at this story again.

Judy said, "Answer a few questions for me." I'd like you to take out a pen or pencil and a sheet of paper to answer those questions yourself. You can answer true, false, or unanswered in this story.

Here are Judy's questions:
1. A man appeared after the owner had turned off the shop lights.
2. The robber was a man.
3. The man did not demand money.
4. The person who opened the cash register was the owner.
5. The owner scooped up the contents of the cash register and ran away.
6. Someone opened the cash register.
7. After the man who demanded money scooped up the contents of the cash register, he ran away.
8. While the cash register contained money, the story does not say how much.
9. The robber demanded money from the owner.
10. The story concerns a series of events which only refers to three people. The owner of the store, a man who demanded money, and a member of the police force.

One of the best ways to persuade others is with your ears — by listening to them.

– Dean Rusk

Let's find out how you did. The correct answers are:

1. Unanswered
2. Unanswered
3. False
4. True
5. Unanswered
6. True
7. Unanswered
8. Unanswered
9. Unanswered
10. Unanswered

How did you do? Did you get them all right? Half? My audiences average three. 3!

I hope this experience makes you a little more skeptical about how we pay attention. And you didn't just listen to this story, you read it – twice. For listeners it's a lot worse. In that role, our natural impatience becomes a factor. We complete people's sentences for them. We complete their thoughts for them. And we know a heck of a lot more about what they want than they do. *We are horrific listeners!* We listen to someone speaking at 250 words a minute, yet we think at a rate of a thousand words a minute. We're thinking about what we did yesterday, what we're going to do today. We think about the features and benefits of our products and services. We think about everything but what the person right in front of us is saying.

> *When the other fellow takes a long time he's slow.*
> *When I take a long time I'm thorough.*
> **– John Maxwell**

My suggestion is this: Listen Until It Hurts. Listen until you think to yourself, "I can't listen to this person another second!" Listening is a contact sport. You listen with your eyes. You listen with your face. You listen with your ears. You listen with your body. And you listen with a pen or pencil if necessary, and write down every word. Note taking is a flattering gesture, almost always taken as a sign of your regard for the other person's words and your determination to retain them. As Steven Covey says, if you want to have influence with someone they must first feel they have influence with you.

No man would listen to you talk if he didn't know it was his turn next.
– Edgar Watson Howe

It is imperative that we become better listeners, with a system of inquiry at our disposal to probe each prospective customer. Studies have revealed that after one minute we only remember half of what we just heard, and after one day only 25 percent. In order to combat this, I have developed a questioning system that will profoundly improve your effectiveness as a resource person. To help you remember it (or maybe to help me remember) I use the letters of my surname: W-I-L-E-Y. This way, you will have a memory-link.

- **W**: The first question is simply, "What's happening in your world?" You don't want to sound ignorant by walking into a furniture factory and saying, "Oh, do you make chairs here?" Make your question global in scope, a question that indicates your desire to find out what issues are affecting their business life. When you ask what's happening in their world, if they run off on a tangent about something in their personal life, so be it. Listen until it hurts. But at least ask for a Cliffs Notes description about what's going on in their world. Then listen intently to what they say, as if your life depended on it.
- **I**: "In what areas are you having difficulty?" is up next. If you prefer to phrase it with a more positive emphasis, then ask, "In what areas do you see the most room for improvement?" Now that you know what's going on in the customer's world, you need to discover the problem areas. Again, listening closely to the response is key. By allowing them to dictate the pace of the interaction you are both securing information and showing your respect for them.

- **L**: "Let me know how these areas that need improvement are hindering you." I understand what's going on in your world, I understand in what areas you're having difficulty. But I'd like to understand how those difficult areas are affecting you on a corporate, personal, or any other level.
- **E**: "Envision yourself wielding a magic wand. How would you fix your problem?" The follow up to this question is "How will you recognize when it is fixed?" I mean, how many times have you solved a client's problem and the client didn't even recognize that it was fixed? You want to know up front what has to happen for that person to see that you have solved his or her problem.
- **Y**: I know – you're hoping that Y will stand for "Yes, I can help you! My solution, my product, my service is just what the doctor ordered. It chops, it slices, it dices, it's just what you want." We wish life were that easy, but the fact is that "yes I can help you with my products or services" only happens about five percent of the time – if you're lucky. But sales professionals typically try to force it to happen the majority of the time. A much more effective way to handle this would be to say, "I understand what's happening in your world. I know in which areas you're having difficulty. I know what those areas of difficulty are doing to you in your world, and I know how you would fix it if you could. I've got to be honest with you. I wish I could help you, but I don't think I can. But I'll tell you what I am going to do. I'm going to put some time and effort into finding help for you. I used to work at another firm [or I used to work in that other field, whatever]. I think I may know where to get you help, and I am going to try to obtain that help because I want to be a resource for you."
- If your product partially solves the customer's problem then another option is "Yes, I can help you in one or two of these areas, but not all of them. So let me help you in the areas where I can and I promise I will put time and effort into helping you get the solution for the others." Presented with a refreshing attitude like that, your clients will remember you forever. You helped them and it wasn't in a self-serving capacity. You just found them help because you cared and treated them as you would a friend.

We all have a particularly cherished friend. Sit back in your chair right now and imagine the telephone rings, and it's that good friend.

"How are you doing?"

"I've got to bring my daughter to school and pick up my son, I'm really in a jam. I need a car!"

Do you think ... hmmmmm, maybe I can rent Randy my car for $60 a day? No, of course not. Do you think, maybe I can send Randy down to the local car lot and he'll buy a car and I can get a commission? Surely not. The only thing you think is, how can I help Randy? I can lend him my car. If I can't lend him my car, maybe my sister's car is available.

If you treat your clients that way, you can cultivate the same kind of bond, the same kind of relationship, the same kind of interaction that you have with your close friends. Think of making sales calls in the manner of making a few friends today. You want to enter into a few partnerships today. So when you're asking the second question of the WILEY questioning series, "In what areas are you having problems?" don't be self-serving and phrase it like, "In what areas are you having problems with the two-cylinder widget that I happen to sell?"

If you are successful in questioning the WILEY way three magical things will happen. First, your clients, friends or partners will give you constant feedback, and as Ken Blanchard noted in *The One Minute Manager,* "Feedback is the breakfast of champions." They'll do that because you helped them out last time-and with no personal gain. They'll remember that forever.

Second, they'll recommend you passionately. You know, recommendations are still essential in business. The problem is, the days are over where three good references mean anything at all. Serial killers can come up with three good references. You want more than a reference. You want someone to *recommend you passionately.* While I'm in my office in Gettysburg, Pennsylvania, I have to count on the fact that someone in Seattle is talking to someone in Baltimore and saying, "You should hire Steve Wiley." And not just by saying, "Steve Wiley is a good speaker. You should have him come to your National Sales Meeting." That isn't enough! I need recommendations like, "You mean to tell me you're considering Steve Wiley for your National

Sales Meeting, and you haven't booked him yet? Well, you'd better hurry up or you'll miss out on a wonderful presentation, and that would really be a tragedy for your people!" *That kind of recommendation makes all the difference in the world.*

Third, and here's the kicker, they will forgive you when you screw up! I don't think anyone reading this book can claim to live a life free of flaws. If you do, I'd like to know who you are. The fact is that, we're all going to screw up. And wouldn't it be great if your client not only understood, but forgave you for that?

We all make mistakes, and I can assure you I'm no exception. One time I was making a presentation, standing on a big stage with a curtain behind me. When I address a large audience I move around quite a lot. On this particular day, I mistakenly thought that there was a wall behind the back curtain. In fact, the curtain marked the end of the platform and there was nothing behind it but air. Air – and a five-foot drop onto a concrete floor! So at a certain point in the speech, to emphasize a point, I jumped back expecting to hit the wall behind me. But when all I hit was a curtain, I began to fall backwards. Reflexively, I grabbed the curtain and held onto the fabric for a split second, probably at a 45° angle, then luckily was able to pull myself upright. All this in full view of the audience. Well, they were startled at first, but after I made a few jokes about it, they willingly forgave me and offered a warm round of applause at the end of the speech.

A passionate recommendation from a former client to a potential client is a major time saver, and our *time* is the scarcest resource of all. A few years back a large company commissioned an expensive and extensive study of the time management skills of 400 of their sales representatives. The results were incredible! Over 57 percent of the time, sales professional dealt with administrative work – filling out forms, making requests. An additional 29 percent of their time was spent traveling to and from the customer, either on an airplane, in a car or on foot. Think about those findings for a second. My goodness, if 57 percent of their time is spent doing administrative work, and 29 percent is spent going to and from customers, that leaves only 14 percent of their time to actually spend in front of their customers.

If that were not bad enough, the study found that only 25 percent of that 14 percent was spent actually speaking to the customer about purchasing something. Then the really bad news: only 10 percent of the 25 percent of the 14 percent of the time did these sales representatives receive a "yes." I don't know if you had your calculator out as you were reading this, but that comes out to less than one-half of one percent of the time that these sales professionals were scoring for their company.

Can a company make it on a hit ratio of 0.5 percent? This one sure didn't feel like it could. The company saw the study results and hit the panic button. It started to computerize more of its office operations so its sales representatives didn't have to fill out as many forms, or mail as many forms or be on the telephone as long. The company mounted a tremendous effort and in so doing knocked that 57 percent administrative work time down to about 51 percent. Turning to the 29 percent travel time, it reorganized territories. The company got out the maps and reconfigured the entire sales effort geographically throughout the country. So it knocked the 29 percent down to 21 percent. Then they did the math: This only improved the hit ratio by about 0.25 percent. Can we increase sales by boosting the time we spend in front of the customer? Well, yes, but it is limited by intractable natural obstacles.

Think about this for a solution: What if you had some of your customer friends, your partners, recommending you passionately. Wouldn't that be great? If I had to count on being in Boston, being in Des Moines, being in San Francisco saying, "May I speak for you?" I wouldn't have any business. The WILEY questioning method allows us to work with a different clock.

Chapter 6 — Yes, *if...*

He that complies against his will is of his own opinion still.
– Samuel Butler

*Remember that a person's name is to that person the sweetest
and most important sound in any language.*
– Dale Carnegie

We now have a little consultative selling and a little leadership under our belts. You've created relationships, you've created followship, and you have a personal mission. Now let's get down to the blocking and tackling of persuasion, the details of how we make it work. How do I write this contract? How many of my products is the customer going to buy? So let's talk a little bit about influence, because once you have cultivated a customer relationship, you have to actually affect the contract.

We have to decide the how much, the when, and the where of the order. This is an area where the ability to influence others really pays off. If you can get your way more often, will that be good for you? Sure! I want you to be able to create followship and become a more effective leader and resource professional. But I also want you to be able to get your way more often. Wouldn't that be fun? Here are a few tips, *a la* Father Guido Sarducci, to help you get your way more often.

Do you remember Father Guido? He was an Italian priest portrayed by Don Novello, most famously on *Saturday Night Live*. I know a lot about Italians. My aunt's names are Bina, Rena, Gena, Pena, Tina, and Maria. Seriously. Father Sarducci said that he was going to start a "Five-a-Minute-a University." He was going to teach in just five minutes everything a college graduate remembers five years after graduation. While this was a comedic sketch, he had a great point, because here I am trying to teach you about consultative selling, leadership, productivity, and influence in a book that can be read in a few hours.

Guido would say, "Okay, we're going to start the five-a minute university right now. We got to have a science. Physics, physics, okay. We only got about nine seconds for physics class, so I can only teach you one thing. *What goes up must come down. That's it!* Now you go away to college and take physics 101, 102, 201, 202, and five years later what do you remember about physics? What goes up must come down. Now, we also should have a business course. Because every-one's going to grow up, get a job and buy a car. And we should have a business course. "Economics!" he'd screech. "Okay we only gotta fourteen seconds for economics class. So we can only learn one thing: *Buy low, sell high.* You'd be surprised at how many people screw thatta one up." What a great routine. You should hear his plan for spring break.

Father Sarducci style, we're just going to give you the highlights on persuasion. Why? Because a study out of Carnegie Mellon University shows that when adults only have to focus on a few concepts their enjoyment is higher, and they are more likely to remember the main points a year, even five later. So we're not going to go into all of persuasion. There are a hundred books on persuasion and negotiation that we can avoid thanks to Father Guido.

We have a global economy now. Let's begin by asking ourselves how we, as Americans, are doing in the area of business influence. You guessed it: horribly! The only reason we've gotten our way is because we have more money and resources than almost anyone else. The company lost $1.1 million last quarter? That's too bad, maybe we'll do better next quarter. Let's go to lunch. After that we'll throw some more resources at the problem. Assign a few more vice presidents to the project and let them do some "blamestorming," that'll do it.

Until recently, all we've had to come up with are more corporate resources, and they seemed unlimited. I don't care if you're with Intel, Xerox, or Orange County, California, we no longer have endless resources of money, time, people, and things. So we've got to get better at influencing other people to strike a more favorable deal with us. Welcome to the new millennium!

The number one thing you and I should do differently when we want to sell something is to stop requesting the *fair* price. A predetermined concept of *fairness* or idea of what each side *should* accept really hampers your results. Oh, you should have a goal in mind. Just don't open your discussion by tossing your goal on the table and saying, "This is fair." In some parts of the world it baffles the locals how something could be *fair* before any haggling takes place. Since America is a melting pot of world influences, you cannot assume that your counterpart will buy into your unique notion of what is fair before you have attempted to trade back and forth a bit.

Stop opening at your desired goal. Say you have an automobile you want to sell. It's worth about $10,000. You'd be happy to get $10,000 for it. In fact your spouse saw two of them across town at $10,000 a piece. Your neighbor works for the National Auto Dealers Association and he tells you that's a very good price. You call your banker and say, "I want to sell that thing in my garage." She says, "That will be fine, but you've got to pay the $10,000 loan." So let's think about it. You have to get $10,000 for the car; you'd be happy with $10,000, because it is a fair price.

So you put an ad in the local newspaper offering to sell your car for $10,000. Someone calls and offers $8,000. What do you have to say? "No, I need $10,000 because my wife, my banker, my neighbor blah, blah, blah." And if you're lucky, the next thing they'll say is, "How about $9,000?" Once again, you have to say, "No, I need $10,000. Did I tell you the reasons why? Blah, blah, blah." If you're real lucky the caller will offer $9,500. Once again, you tell him, "No, I need $10,000 and these are the reasons why, in case you didn't hear me the first two times." What happens next? Click, he hangs up. Click, negotiations break down between owners and the players. *Click*, negotiations break down between the two countries. *Click*, negotiations break down between Caterpillar and the union. It happens all the time.

Poor negotiators figure out in advance what they want and they ask for it. Good negotiators figure out what they want and ask for *more*. Why do they ask for more? Because they're greedy? They ask for more so they can give away some ground!

Before you enter into another business interaction, where you want to persuade someone to do something your way, first take the time to decide what the heck it is you want. Many times people fare poorly in a negotiation because they do not bother to figure out beforehand what it is they want. You may have fallen into this trap. It's common; I've done it too many times. So before you enter into your next interaction, figure out what you want. When you know what you want, call that desired position your **target outcome**. It can be a target date, a target quantity, a target time, whatever. But it's the outcome you prefer, if the discussions go reasonably well.

Next, before you begin talking, use your intelligence, your experience, your knowledge, and your due diligence to come up with a **more** aggressive **position**. Come up with a stiff request that is not what you would expect to receive, but which is at least arguably reasonable, and *begin there*. Now, do you start high in order to have an argument? No, you start high so you can give ground and make the other party feel good about wresting concessions from us. When the other side can show something they will feel as if they've done well – which they will have. People in our "fair-minded" society have trouble with this, more than you would think. If you persuade yourself to start high, you're halfway home, even before the discussion takes place.

When you give ground, do it in small increments. People often think, "That guy Steve says I should ask for more than $10,000 for my car. I don't feel good about that, I feel like I need to take a shower after this, but I'll do it. I've done some research and $12,000 would be reasonable for a pristine car of that model and year. Pristine is something my car is not. But okay, I'm asking twelve thousand." They start high, but the other party says, "Can't you do any better than that?" They say, "Sure, I'll take ten thousand," and they are right back at the *fair* position, and now they have to say no if the other side asks for more concessions. Keep making concessions, just make them small, so you can make them more often.

In every one of these interactions, the other side is going to ask you for something. Can I start later? Can you finish it earlier? Can I pay less? Can you give me more? They're going to ask you for something, without fail. So think about it: when you ask someone to give in during a negotiation, what do you want to hear? You want to hear the word "yes." Think about what happens when you muster the courage to ask someone for a concession, hoping to hear "yes," and the answer is "no." What happens to the climate? It becomes cold, antagonistic; a chill descends. So, let me see, when I ask people for something and I want them to say yes, maybe that means when people ask *me* for something, maybe *they* want *me* to say yes! If you start with a higher position, you have room to say yes.

Am I suggesting that you should say yes to every request? No, your company would go out of business with each deal, one by one. All I'm saying is that you have another alternative. Here's an example. I stayed at a Hyatt Regency at Chicago O'Hare several years ago, and I paid $220 for the room. In the morning I went down to the front desk and asked whether I could please have another key to my room. The very pleasant desk person looked at me and said, "No." She may as well have jumped across the desk and punched me in the face. "Thank you for staying with us and spending your $220, but NO." Now, why did she say no? Frankly, she had a reason, because it was eight a.m. and I had already lost two keys to my room. So the third time she felt justified in saying no. But I made a suggestion to her in a very pleasant way. I suggested that instead of saying, "No, you can't have another key," she could have said, "Yes, Mr. Wiley, we can give you another key to your room, *if* you allow the bellman to follow you up to the room, and you give him the two keys you already lost this morning, you idiot you." The only thing I would have heard was "YES." Well maybe I would have heard "you idiot," too, but I swear it wouldn't have bothered me.

Other people simply don't like to hear you say no. If someone asks you for a favor, instead of saying no, try to think creatively. Think of a way to say, "Yes *if*." Yes, we could drop the price ten percent *if* you buy two of them. Yes, we could do that *if* you waited until next quarter to take delivery. Yes, we could do that *if* you take the blue ones. Yes, we could do that *if* we remove color altogether. "Yes, *if*" is light years ahead of saying *no*. Does it work all the time? No, it doesn't work all the time. But, my goodness, it will work most of the time.

You can even use it to lighten the mood, to add some humor to a potentially aggravating situation. A friend of mine is in charge of advertising at a newspaper. A customer called him and said, "Scott, I love your paper and I want to advertise next month. Last month you gave me a 15 percent discount. Is it possible I can have an 84 percent discount this month?" And Scott was thinking, "Oh, jeez. I took that class from Steve Wiley and I'm supposed to say 'Yes, *if*.'" So he stammered, "Yes, if, er, yes, if I were *stupid* I could do that."

You can't say yes to everything and anything. Supply and demand will always overrule these tips. But "yes, *if*" will get you a long, long way.

Always be aware of your ego throughout this process. Be aware of your own false ideas about competition. Be aware of your instinct to win, because those instincts, John Wayne, and all the sports programs you ever watched or played, teach you that the other side must lose in order for you to win. This stuff requires patience to be done right. And you're thinking, "I don't have time to be patient." Is that true, or is it that patience never gets priority in our busy world?

To sum up the art of persuasion, figure out what you want before you enter into an interaction. Start with a more aggressive position so that you can give ground, and therefore the other side can feel that they are doing well. And always know your bottom line before the interaction begins. Say "yes, *if*" instead of no. Say "yes, *if*" instead of yes. And make concessions, but make sure they're small concessions.

Pickett's Charge: A Broken Negotiation
by Jared Peatman

At the beginning of their classic *Getting to Yes,* authors Roger Fisher and William Ury note that we are all negotiators, every single day. But as Steve points out, most of us lack an actual method for negotiations. In our daily work lives most of us probably deal with internal colleagues more than folks on the outside, and it seems downright mercenary to approach our interactions with them as a negotiation: after all, we are both supposed to be working together. But what happens when we become convinced that a colleague or boss is taking the organization down the wrong path? How do we implement Steve's negotiating and persuading tactics to convince them to change their plan? To bring this question alive, how might our world today be a different place had Confederate General James Longstreet used these techniques to persuade his boss, Robert E. Lee, to rethink the attack we call Pickett's Charge? [See image on pages 56-57.]

On the morning of July 3, 1863, Robert E. Lee faced a pivotal decision. Two days earlier his army had encountered and thoroughly whipped approximately a third of the Union's Army of the Potomac. On July 2 Lee's attacks made progress but they could not move the Army of the Potomac from its strong defensive position. Lee initially planned to attack both ends of the Union line on July 3, and gave the appropriate orders. But by the time James Longstreet arrived to confer with Lee, the commander had changed his mind and pointing toward the Union line, announced he would send an attack force of 15,000 men across a mile-wide open field to strike the center of the enemy army.

Longstreet was incredulous, noting later, "I felt then that it was my duty to express my convictions; I said, 'General, I have been a soldier all my life. I have been with soldiers engaged in fights by couples, by squads, companies, regiments, divisions, and armies, and should know, as well as any one, what soldiers can do. It is my opinion that no fifteen thousand men every arranged for battle can take that position.'" To Longstreet's chagrin, Lee replied, "The enemy is there, and I am going to strike him." In his memoirs Longstreet noted, "Nothing was left but to proceed." Of the fifteen thousand men who began that charge, half ended up killed, wounded, or captured in what has to be described as one of the worst decisions of the war.

What Longstreet needed was a way to negotiate with his boss to persuade him that there were better alternatives. What would it look like if Longstreet had employed the method Steve outlined for us? Let's review Steve's advice:

- A predetermined concept of *fairness* hampers your results.
- Figure out your *target outcome* ahead of time.
- Ask for *more* than your target outcome, but not outrageously so.
- Make several *small* concessions.
- Determine your *bottom line* ahead of time.
- Say "*Yes, if*" rather than just "yes" or just "no."
- Be aware of your *ego*.

Now put yourself in Longstreet's shoes. There was no issue of fairness here, so we can skip that question. Did Longstreet identify a *targeted outcome* ahead of time? Yes and no. He encouraged Lee to move around to the right of the Union Army and take up a position nearer Washington D.C., forcing the enemy to attack. But Longstreet had been making that argument for three days to no avail. It was stale at this point, and thus an ineffective target.

Did Longstreet *ask for a bit more* than his targeted outcome so he then had room to make small concessions? No, and actually he failed in two ways here. First, Longstreet asked for exactly what he wanted, and consequently had no room to maneuver when Lee said no. Second, he knew from the past three days that what he was asking for was, in Lee's mind, outrageous. Asking Lee to disengage and move his entire army is similar to the example we used earlier of Steve's boys asking to go to the library… in Rome. It was outside the limits of reality.

Steve encourages us to know our bottom line ahead of time. The aforementioned Fisher and Ury suggest knowing your **BATNA: B**est **A**lternative **T**o a **N**egotiated **A**greement. When a negotiated outcome becomes less desirable than that BATNA, it is time to walk away. Longstreet did not establish either. When Lee put his foot down, Longstreet gave in. Some would argue that in a military hierarchy Longstreet would have been insubordinate to continue resisting Lee's plan. But remember that the result of this decision was 7,500 casualties, and ask whether Longstreet had a duty to those men to continue trying to change Lee's mind. For Lee's part, he should have remembered Henry Jomini's warning, "To commit the execution of a purpose to one who disapproves of the plan of it, is to employ but one-third of the man; his heart and his head are against you; you have command only of his hands." How might things have been different if Longstreet stuck to his bottom line and protested more vehemently?

The central part of Steve's advice is his suggestion to respond, "Yes, *if...*" rather than "no" or "yes" whenever possible. Longstreet commented to others on the battlefield that he thought an assault force of 30,000 would succeed. Why did he not say: "Yes, General Lee, I feel confident we can make that assault, break the Union line, win the battle, and possibly force the enemy to sue for peace, *if* you give me just two more divisions." This idea was in Longstreet's head, the extra troops were available, so why did he not say "Yes, *if...*?" Lee had repeatedly shown he was all in for this battle, and it seems his normally cautious general asking him to be even bolder would have caused him to give serious thought to Longstreet's proposal. In *The Way of the Owl* author Frank Rivers notes that wise owls stay at the negotiating table even when they know the outcome may not favor them because they realize they still might be able to shape the outcome in a way to make it somewhat less offensive. If Longstreet responded *yes, if* you can give me 30,000 troops, Lee might have had a counteroffer, but at least both sides would still be at the negotiating table.

Finally, Longstreet does not appear to have controlled his *ego* in this situation. When Lee rejected his advice Longstreet withdrew from the conversation. This could have been due to a bruised ego or sorrow over what he predicted would happen. But if it was due to the second cause Longstreet should have found other people to convince Lee: whether that was the artilleryman who would oversee the cannonade that was to precede the charge, or the other corps commander whose men would be involved, or the engineer who had ridden the ground that morning. That Longstreet did not ask any of these other men to speak with Lee suggests that he felt if he could not convince Lee then no one could. Either way you read the situation, Longstreet's ego got in the way.

In his magnificent *The Courageous Follower* author Ira Chaleff contends that the most powerful tool a follower has is the ability to persuade. If Longstreet had used Steve's method on that July morning a century and a half ago, how might things have been different?

Reflection — Yes, *if...*

Our strategic purpose here is not to preach at you, but simply to encourage you to think and reflect about your own leadership. Towards that end, the following questions might be useful.

Reflect...

- What are my normal negotiating tactics? Do I have a plan when entering a negotiation?

- What was the outcome of my last negotiation?

- What could I have done better?

- How many of the seven steps Steve outlined do I routinely employ?

... and Apply

Think about an upcoming situation where you anticipate needing to negotiate.

- Do I know what my target outcome and bottom line are?

- What opportunities might I have to say "Yes, if..."

- In what ways might my ego get in the way of a successful negotiation?

- Which of the seven steps is most likely to present me with problems?

Chapter 7 — You Can't Lead From the Grave

Happiness lies, first of all, in health.
– George William Curtis

The whole area of personal productivity takes for granted that we'll be feeling well, mentally and physically. People who are crabby, tired, unfocused, sick, moody, or irritable are not productive. I don't care who we are, we're just not productive. Now rest easy as you read this: I'm not going to tell you to eat fruits and vegetables and exercise more. We all know that right?

A great friend from college experimented with every recreational pharmaceutical there was. The guy was a drug addict, plain and simple. Ten years after college we ran into each other and I said, "How are you doing?" He said, "I tell you I've been through hell. I've lost a couple of wives, a few houses, several cars, a dozen jobs, and spent $40,000 on drug rehabilitation. Then Ronald Reagan gets elected; his wife, Nancy, goes on this war against drugs; and I find out after all that, I could have just said no!"

There's a lot more to it, isn't there? My friend knew he shouldn't take drugs. But it wasn't going to help him to have someone telling him not to do it. Likewise, we don't need someone to tell us to eat more fruits and vegetables. We know we should do that. We know it's better than eating a lot of sugar and high fat. What we need is someone to tell us *how* to do that.

I was in a similar situation twenty years ago. Before I could get better at leading and selling, I had to get well. I was 50 pounds overweight and even with two kinds of medication my blood pressure was still 180 over 115 on a good day, and I know you understand the significance of numbers like those.

So I decided I needed to get myself well. It's just like when you get on a commercial airline and the safety crew has that announcement, "In the event of an emergency, if you're traveling with a small child (or a business associate who is acting like a small child), please put the oxygen mask on yourself first, then the small child." The first time I heard that announcement I was traveling with my three sons, and I thought, "That doesn't make any sense. If we're in an emergency situation I'm going to want to put the oxygen mask on my boys first." But the airline understands I'd be unable to help anybody else if I passed out. It's the same thing I'm talking about here. I had to get well in order to regain control over my business affairs.

What made the most profound impact on my adult life, regarding my health, was my experiences at the Pritikin Longevity Centers located in Miami Beach, Florida, and Santa Monica, California. I urge you to give them a call to receive further information. Their number is 1-855-228-2818.

It takes about twenty years for the effects of a lifestyle (and this includes diet) to catch up with you. After that, it begins to take its toll. People have heart bypass operations, chemotherapy and all sorts of sad medical interventions. And yet we all know we shouldn't eat certain things, don't we?

Let me borrow your imagination for a minute, and an excerpt from Nathan Pritikin's book. Visualize a society in which everyone loved arsenic. They sprinkled it into their coffee, they stirred it into their soup, they baked it into their bread, they grilled their meat with it. It was the most sought-after food enhancer. They couldn't imagine preparing food without it. But people were getting sick. They got stomachaches, they got headaches. Their hair fell out, their teeth fell out. They started to drop dead at the lunch table and on the golf course. And the rumor went around that maybe it was due to the arsenic. So the pharmaceutical companies started to combat it by coming out with pills for headaches, pills for stomachaches. The dental profession came out with better false teeth. The hair restoration society came out with better wigs. But people kept getting sick, and they kept dropping dead.

One 40-year-old man was sicker than most. The doctor said, "You know, you're not going to make it; you won't live more than a week or two. You'd better have your children come say goodbye." Now this patient was a bright man, and he was a researcher. He had researched other societies that didn't eat arsenic and discovered that those people got sick far less often. So he decided then and there to stop eating arsenic, and he turned down the tray of food brought to him by the hospital, requesting arsenic-free meals after that.

The results were miraculous. So he started publishing papers, reporting, "I stopped eating arsenic and I got better." And the next thing you know, the dairy association came out with 98 percent arsenic-free milk. Cookie companies came out with one-third less arsenic in their cookies. But people kept getting sick.

Now this is not an episode from the *Twilight Zone*. And we're not talking about arsenic. We're talking about our own society, and we're talking about fat, cholesterol, and salt. And the sick person in the story was Nathan Pritikin, the founder of the Pritikin Longevity Center. His son Robert, a good friend of mine, continues his work. Nathan Pritikin was the first person to link cholesterol and fat to heart disease. This was in 1976. In 1985, *60 Minutes* did a big story on him, and everybody found out about his work.

Today, you can't listen to the radio or watch television without someone talking about the dangers of eating too much fat or the benefits of exercise. We are bombarded with guilt for adopting a Western diet of affluence that is killing us. How about this factoid: the first sugar refineries in Europe were built at the behest of Napoleon just two hundred years ago. At that time sugar was expensive and difficult to obtain, so the average European consumed just seven pounds of it each year. Then, the Industrial Revolution and better transportation brought cheap sugar to nearly everyone. The result? Today, the average American consumes over 150 pounds of sugar a year, *over twenty times as much* as the people in Napoleon's time.

Our concern about the damage we are doing via the knife and fork has given birth to a whole new industry. We've got Jenny Craig, we've got Weight Watchers, we've got the grapefruit diet, we've got the South Beach diet. We have former professional athletes crying on television and bald ladies screaming at us. We have never had more of an emphasis on diet in the history of our world. But yet we're fatter and sicker than we've ever been.

City Slickers was a great movie, partially because of the scene where Billy Crystal offers a cynical view of aging to his son's fourth grade class: "Enjoy this time in your life, children, because you'll spend your twenties wondering where your teens went. You'll spend your thirties wondering where your twenties went. In your forties you'll grow a pot belly, lose some hair, and the music will start getting louder. In your fifties you'll have an operation (you'll call it a procedure, but it's an operation). The music will keep getting louder, but you won't mind because you can't hear it as well. In your sixties you'll retire to Ft. Lauderdale, start eating dinner at three in the afternoon, lunch at ten in the morning, and breakfast the night before. And in your seventies you'll start walking around malls eating frozen yogurt and saying, 'Why don't the grandchildren call?' In your eighties you'll fall in love with a Jamaican nurse whom your wife hates but you call 'Mama.' Any questions??"

Billy Crystal verbalized our perception that as we get older, we naturally get sicker, weaker, less productive, and then we die. But it doesn't have to be that way. Television is on so much that the average American will watch nearly a million commercials in our lifetime! Unfortunately two-thirds of those commercials will tell us to eat or drink more of the wrong thing. And they always depict people having a good time. Think about it. You're sitting on your couch at home. You're overweight, you're crabby and you're drinking a soda – and there's a commercial on TV advertising the same drink. But the actors have bikinis on. They're good looking women, good looking men; they're sky diving, they're roller blading, they're having a wonderful time. So you look at your soda, you look at your TV, you look back at your soda and you think, "Hey, maybe I'm not using enough ice."

So we make lifestyle choices even though twenty years later they give us high blood pressure, adult onset diabetes, obesity, heart disease, and several forms of cancer. You don't think advertising is powerful? In 1994 the National Cancer Institute spent $400,000 trying to get people to eat more fruits and vegetables. In that same year a leading cereal manufacturer spent $60 *million* advertising a cereal that had the highest sugar and fat content on the market. We wonder why we're having a problem? My goodness.

Can you imagine being in the marketing division of one of those companies, advertising food that's bad for people? I've got a slogan for them. How about a soup that's full of salt and fat. How about this for a slogan: "Mmm-mmm dead." Or how about, "Give us a week, we'll stop your heart" At the same time, we can't blame it all on Madison Avenue. We have created the ultimate irony of nature. The very mechanisms that developed to protect us from nutritional deficiency are now killing us from the diseases resulting from our newfound abundance. But maybe we can turn things around.

Ladies and gentlemen, I lost fifty pounds in 1989 and I've kept it off. Since 1989, I have not taken one beta blocker, not one blood pressure pill, and recently my blood pressure was 120 over 80. How did I do it? Because of my discipline! No, actually, I love to eat, I love ice cream, I love Mexican food, I love life. But with the help of the Pritikin Longevity Centers I found out that this thing we call our body is a very sophisticated biochemical machine that was adapted to ensure the survival of our cavemen ancestors hundreds of thousands of years ago. And guess what? There is no owner's manual for this machine. I have a can opener with a three-page owner's manual, and yet for the most sophisticated machine on earth, I don't have an owner's manual.

Hundreds of thousands of years ago, men and women fueled this machine ten, eleven, or twelve times a day. Today 58 percent of our calories come in one meal. Maybe that wouldn't be in the owner's manual. A hundred thousand years ago 89 percent of our intake was fruit and vegetables. Today most of it is fat and chemicals. Maybe that wouldn't be in the manual. A hundred thousand years ago, we were active all day long digging up potatoes, picking fruit, and running away from mountain lions. Today three-fourths of Americans don't exercise at all. The only reason I'm here, and you're here reading this book, is because our ancestors survived periods of famine. Our prehistoric ancestors were able to crawl into a cave and go for long periods without fresh food. Now how did they do it? They did it because this unbelievable machine had developed the "fat instinct." Today we talk about survival of the fittest, but in Neolithic times it was survival of the fattest.

When winter came, prehistoric people couldn't find fresh food because everything was frozen. They couldn't dig up potatoes, couldn't pick fruit. The calorie reduction signaled to their body that winter was coming. The fat instinct said, "Go get some fat and hang on to it." The biological machine called the body reduced their metabolism so they would be able to store fat.

Not only that, the ingestion of fat triggered a further craving for fat, which in the modern animal kingdom (and in human cases such as the Outback Steakhouse) created a reflex known as *gorging*. This means that eating fat makes you crave more fat. In caveman times, this craving for fat kept people alive throughout the winter, when meals would be severely reduced and days without food were common. In that environment, carrying a little extra fat made good sense.

So what does this evolutionary background mean for me today? Well, we still have that caveman body. When we take in fewer calories, we trigger the fat instinct. Have you ever tried to lose weight by cutting down on calories? I know I have. As soon as you cut down on calories you signal your body that winter is coming, which is like saying to it on a biological level, "Hang onto the fat and go get some more if you can."

To combat this effect, *eat more often*. Don't empty your stomach and trigger the fat instinct. Eat more often so your body doesn't think it's going to starve. After all, is starvation a problem these days? Not really. We've got a few inventions to help us out, like the refrigerator.

So here you are, trying to lose weight, trying to be disciplined about it. Mother Nature says get some fat. You resist, saying, "No, Mother, my discipline will see me through." Who's going to win that battle? Mother Nature, every single time. So eat more often, because if you let yourself get hungry between breakfast and lunch you're going to crave the wrong things. This has nothing to do with willpower. It has nothing to do with whether you're a good person or not. It has nothing to do with discipline. It has everything to do with our biological machine and its fear of starving. Amid the abundance of food in our culture, there are grossly overweight people in America who spend most of their time going from meal to meal, trapped in ballooning bodies that, ironically, fear they are starving!

In prehistoric times when winter came our ancestors cuddled up into a cave, reduced bodily activity and triggered the fat instinct. The body thought, "Uh-oh, winter's here, better slow down the metabolic rate." A study from Princeton University revealed that when we do not exercise, our metabolic rate decreases by a third. What a fix that puts us in! We get fatter, our metabolism declines, yet our bodies want more fatty food. Twenty years of this and we are on the operating table.

The remedy is to take a walk. Don't go out and try to run a marathon right away. People who haven't exercised in fifteen years make a New Year's resolution and say, "OK, I'll go out tomorrow and I'm going to start an exercise program. I think I'll jog to L.A. and back." And they sprain an ankle and don't exercise for six more weeks. You don't have to join a gym and start power lifting. Just go take a walk.

Start simply by taking a walk every day; you're signaling your body that springtime is here. Hey Metabolism, everything is coming up roses. *Burn baby burn.* Then you won't crave fat as much.

> *The sovereign invigorator of the body is exercise,*
> *and of all the exercises walking is the best.*
> **– Thomas Jefferson**

In summary, if you eat more often, your body won't be afraid of starving. You won't need as many calories. If you take a walk, your body will think it's springtime and your metabolic rate will increase. It's that simple!

Here is another health tip for you. What's the third leading cause of absenteeism in America today? Not going to work? Yeah, that will do it every time! But really, it's lower-back pain. We lose $38 billion and ten million work days in lost time in America every year because of lower back pain. What's the leading cause of lower-back pain? Weakening stomach muscles.

This doesn't have to be. At Cornell University people in their seventies, eighties, and nineties tripled the strength in their stomach after just six weeks of situps. The first time I tried to do a sit-up after not exercising for ten years I could barely get my head off the ground. But after about a week I could do a few of them comfortably. After a couple of weeks, I could do several.

It's the afternoon and you are on the phone making outgoing marketing calls. What's on your mind? Food! Are you at your best? Heck no! You protest, "Steve, I'm a professional." I don't care. First of all you're an animal, and animals have cravings. You say, "I have discipline to overcome my cravings." Baloney.

So please make it a regular point to eat breakfast. Then eat small healthy meals often throughout the day. Take a walk and do some situps. I do these things daily and I feel marvelous.

Some people lose their health getting wealthy
and then lose their wealth getting healthy.
– Unknown

Reflection — You Can't Lead From the Grave

Our strategic purpose here is not to preach at you, but just to encourage you to think and reflect about your own leadership. Toward that end, the following questions might be useful:

Reflect...

Use the WILEY questioning method to think about your health.

- What is the current state of my health?

- In what areas is my health causing me difficulty?

- Let us reflect about the ways that area is hindering you.

and Apply...

- Envision yourself wielding a magic wand: how would you fix the problem area/areas?

- Yes, we can work on this!

    - What can I do this week to start making a difference?

    - What can I do next week to build upon that slight change?

    - Where do I want to be a month from now?

Chapter 8 — The Pope and the Colonel

In urging you to adopt the tips I've presented in this book, I want to emphasize that I have the utmost respect for what you do. I just hope I haven't come across as a know-it-all. Nobody likes a know-it-all, whether a speaker, an author, a mother-in-law, a policeman, or a barber or hairdresser.

I had a friend, Charlie, who hated his barber because he was such a darn know-it-all. His wife said, "We're about to go to Europe, you've got to get your hair cut." He said, "I don't want to do that, I hate the barber." But she made him go.

He sat down in the chair and his barber said, "Hey Charlie, what are you doing this summer?"

Charlie said, "I'm going to go on vacation."

"You don't want to go on vacation, summer is a bad time. Where are you going?

"I'm going to Europe."

"Oh, what a silly thing to do, it's expensive. Where are you going in Europe?"

"I'm going to Italy."

"Italy, ahh, it's going to be hot and crowded. What are you going to do in Italy?"

"Well, I'm going to try to see the Pope."

"Ha, ha, see the Pope, yeah, right. He will look like a tiny ant on the balcony. There'll be ten thousand pushy Italians around you. Have a good time!"

Charlie said, "I hate that barber."

He went on vacation and he came back. He needed another haircut. He walked into the barbershop and the barber said, "Did you go on vacation yet? Was it expensive like I told you?"

"Yeah."

"Was Italy hot and crowded like I told you it would be?"

"Yeah, it was."

"Did you see the Pope? Was it just like I told you?"

"Yeah," said Charlie suddenly, "Except when the Pope talked to me."

The barber said, "The Pope talked to you?"

"Yup, it was just like you predicted. He was just a tiny ant on the balcony. But then he came down on the piazza and walked through ten thousand people, and came right up to me."

The barber couldn't believe his ears. "What did the Pope say to you?" he demanded.

"He came up and he grabbed me by the back of the head and said, 'Who the devil cuts your hair?'"

Every salesperson has a funny story about their most interesting sales call. Mine happened several years ago. We were in the business of doing oil changes on premise. We would go to companies like Federal Express and ask if we could change the oil in their vehicles during the night so they could use the trucks all day. So my most terrific salesperson, Terry Smith, and I went to Fort Meade, Maryland, to pitch the base on servicing all its vehicles. There was a new colonel there, and he was fooling with the speakerphone option.

We waited outside until we heard him say, "Send those guys in." So we entered the office and met him. He was a big man, really huge. We sat down nervously, and we did features and benefits, features and benefits, features and benefits.

And he said, "Okay, I'll give you a trial. You can service one of the motor pools and if it works well, we'll let you do more of them."

He leaned over and pressed the speaker button and we heard, "Motor Pool."

"Yeah, how many vehicles do we have down there in section 9?"

The voice on the intercom said, "Uh, 14 half-tracks, 6 jeeps and a Cadillac for that new fat ass colonel."

We gulped. The colonel reddened and yelled, "Do you know who this is?"

The voice said, "Nope."

"This is the Colonel speaking."

There was dead silence. After several long seconds had elapsed, the voice said, "D-do you know who this is, sir?"

"No, I do not."

"Well then, so long, fat ass."

Communication is the key to relationships. Many bestsellers today point out that communication is affected by gender, a subject way beyond the scope of this book, but one for which I naturally have an opinion.

Who's a better communicator, a man or a woman? Women are far better, but I'm going to let men off the hook here: it's not our fault. You see, men and women are built differently. I don't mean in the obvious way, but insofar as our brains have two sides. The left side is task oriented, testosterone driven, wanting to get things done. The right side is creative and patient. All people have both sides. But women, because of differences in their physiological makeup, can communicate back and forth between the two sides a lot better than men can. Women have an eight-lane super highway between the two sides. Guys have a dirt path.

A woman on any given day will use 24,000 words to express herself. A man will use 11,000. One of the problems we have in dual-career households today is that by the time we get home at night the guy has seven words left. The woman has 9,000. She comes home and says, "Hi, how was your day? Wait until I tell you about mine. We got last quarter's figures and we beat the quarter before and the quarter before that. You know that girl that works at the Y? It doesn't matter; she's pregnant. She changed her hair color. And your mother called to say we are invited to go on vacation the second week of August. How was your day?"

He stares at her, glassy-eyed, and says, "Food. Home. Beer. Remote. Sex. Happy. Sleep."

Thank you for reading our book. We hope you had as much fun reading it as we had putting it together, and that you are excited to take action. Until we meet again, best wishes for success and good health in your personal and professional lives.

To laugh often and much; to win the respect of intelligent people and the affection of children; to earn the appreciation of honest critics and endure the betrayal of false friends; to appreciate beauty; to find the best in others; to leave this world a bit better, whether by a healthy child, a garden patch or a redeemed social condition; to know even one life has breathed easier because you have lived. This is to have succeeded.
– Ralph Waldo Emerson